# Planning *a* Future
# *for*
# Your Family's Past

## Second Edition

How to keep your family history safe for future
generations by organizing, curating, writing
instructions, and sharing now!

By **Marian Burk Wood**

Author of the genealogy blog *Climbing My Family Tree*

https://ClimbingMyFamilyTree.blogspot.com/

# CONTENTS

✓ *Prepare* to organize and analyze
✓ *Allocate* ownership by curating
✓ *Set up* a genealogical "will"
✓ *Share* your family's history now

* File your digital files and emails
* Digitize captions
* Back up regularly

# INTRODUCTION TO THE SECOND EDITION

Do you know what will happen to your family's old photos, documents, stories, and heirlooms after you join your ancestors in the years to come? Many family historians are concerned about keeping their genealogy collection safe for the long term, either in the hands of descendants or in the hands of an institution. That's why I developed the four-step **PASS** process, a guide to organizing, analyzing, sharing, and writing instructions so genealogical materials will survive into the future.

## New in this edition

For the second edition, I've written a new chapter about ideas to consider if there are no obvious heirs for your family's history (Chapter 10). Also new: suggestions for safeguarding heirlooms and photos from ancestors without descendants (in Chapters 6 and 7) and ensuring that relatives have key details such as ancestor burial places (see Chapter 8).

In addition, I've included new ideas for sharing family history through bite-sized projects (in Chapter 11). As technology marches on, I've thoroughly updated sections about organizing and digitizing materials (in Chapters 2 and 3) and added new online resources. I've also expanded coverage of how to locate and approach repositories that accept collections or individual artifacts (in Chapter 7). Finally, I've revised the sample inventory, index, and cousin connection forms for easier sorting and searching (in Chapters 4 and 8).

## Overview of PASS

The first step in the process is to **prepare** by getting your genealogy collection in order (Chapters 1-5). The second step is to **allocate** ownership, deciding what to keep and what can leave your collection (Chapters 6-7). The third step is to **set up** instructions for the future of your collection (Chapters 8-10). The fourth step is to **share** your family history, now (Chapter 11).

Even if you think there are no obvious heirs for your genealogical materials, you can take steps today to avoid having your collection wind up in the recycle bin later.

Every chapter ends with a brief listing of key points. This handy feature sums up chapter information and shows at a glance what was covered. Quick and to the point!

Remember this motto: *Life by the inch is a cinch, life by the yard is hard*. Don't try to tackle the whole collection at one time, or you'll become overwhelmed and discouraged. Just work on your plan, a little at a time. Inch by inch, you'll make progress.

## Don't bequeath a genealogical mess

Did you inherit a genealogical mess? I inherited a hodgepodge of family photos, letters, home movies, and other assorted items in battered cardboard boxes. Luckily, my cousin Betty had collected documents and oral histories and had begun to construct a maternal family tree. But on my father's side, I started with just my grandparents' full names and incomplete dates.

My husband's family left a jumble of photo albums, old slide carousels, diaries, World War II memorabilia, and scraps of paper noting ancestors' names. Working with his siblings,  we reconstructed a basic family tree going back a century on both sides, but we needed a lot more detail.

It was only after the genealogy bug bit that I began putting these materials in order and analyzing them. When I picked up an old wedding portrait or a certificate of naturalization that represented an immigrant ancestor's dream come true, I felt like a time-traveler visiting the past.

This inspired me to learn how to organize, inventory, and protect these precious documents, photos, and artifacts for the long term. I'm sharing key items with other family members now, captioning photos, donating selected items to repositories, and passing the rest to the next generation.

As I get organized, I discover clues to my ancestors' past. Some relatives have entrusted me with original family photos to safeguard for the future. I'm also ensuring that ancestors who had no descendants are remembered by including them in my plans. And, to be sure family history lives on, I'm sharing ancestor information on key genealogy websites, with privacy in mind.

## Four steps to PASS

The PASS process, getting your genealogy collection ready to pass to the next generation or outside the family, consists of four steps:

> Step 1: Prepare to organize and analyze (Chapters 1-5)
>
> Step 2: Allocate ownership (Chapters 6-7)
>
> Step 3: Set up a genealogical "will" (Chapters 8-10)
>
> Step 4: Share family history now (Chapter 11)

You can work on these steps in order or choose specific aspects to focus on over time. The key is to begin the process and make progress so your family's history will be safe for the future, whether in the care of a relative or in one or more repositories.

# ABOUT THE AUTHOR

My love of genealogy began in 1998 when the genealogist cousin of my mother's generation asked a basic question: "What do you know about your father's family?" At the time, I knew almost nothing, unfortunately.

In the years since, I've learned a great deal about my father's family and helped my cousin do more research into my mother's family. Best of all, genealogy has brought us closer together and connected us with cousins worldwide. Similarly, researching my husband's family tree, with roots stretching back beyond the Mayflower, has opened new horizons and introduced us to cousins we never knew he had.

In my life before genealogy, I was a marketing executive with an MBA degree from Long Island University and a BA from the City University of New York. After working in financial services and the nonprofit sector, I became a college textbook author.

These days, with family history research and education as my main focus, I specialize in "how-to" presentations and articles. Please see my long-running genealogy blog, *Climbing My Family Tree*, for tips about interesting techniques, ideas for writing family history, the benefits of cousin bait, and more.

-- Marian Burk Wood

https://ClimbingMyFamilyTree.blogspot.com

On Twitter: **@MarianBWood**

# ACKNOWLEDGEMENTS

This second edition is dedicated to cousin Larry Wood, a multi-talented genealogist with an eagle eye for detail. Since we connected on a surname message board more than a decade ago, he has generously shared his extensive knowledge of the Wood family tree and his many ancestor photos. My warmest appreciation to Larry and his wife Maureen for their friendship over the years.

From deep in my heart, I give thanks to my husband Wally Wood, the love of my life. Your encouragement keeps me going—you're always ready with a supportive hug, thoughtful advice, and just the right words.

I am very grateful to my long-time friend Susan Brier, the incredibly gifted graphic designer who created this book's outstanding cover.

Sending hugs to my cherished sis Isabel, my wonderful Burk nieces and nephews, and my fabulous Wood and Biancolo relatives from coast to coast, including my much-loved grandchildren.

Finally, my affectionate greetings to the many cousins who have been part of my genealogy journey. It's been a delight getting to know you as we learn more about the ancestors we share.

*---MBW*

# CHAPTER 1
## ORGANIZED STORAGE FOR YOUR COLLECTION

You already have a collection of materials, whether you're just beginning your research or you inherited a box of old documents, movies, photos, and artifacts. As you begin Step 1 in the PASS process, you'll want to put your collection in order so you can see what you have, access what you want more easily, and analyze individual materials in context.

Keep these questions in mind when planning organized storage:

- How many individual items do you have in your collection?
- What is the age, size, and condition of these items?
- How are you currently organizing and storing your collection?
- Is your collection neat, convenient, and accessible?
- What changes might improve the accessibility, organization, or safety of your collection?

**Investigate options for organized storage**

Before I began organizing my collection, I asked people from local genealogy clubs for advice. It was helpful to hear their comments about different approaches and see their methods in action. I browsed museum, library, and archival sources to understand best practices and, later, asked for suggestions from the genealogy community on social media.

Two helpful online sources to consult are Family Search's page about safely preserving old family photos and ancestral documents (https://tinyurl.com/7r7mfmb8) and this Cyndi's List page with links about the preservation and conservation of older materials (https://cyndislist.com/preservation).

In general, you have three storage options, which can be mixed and matched according to your preferences: (1) files and folders, (2) binders, and (3) boxes (sometimes tubs or plastic tote containers).

## Files and folders

Files and folders (including manila or colored file folders and hanging folders for files) are especially handy for documents, research notes, and other pieces of paper letter size or smaller. If a relative calls with information about an ancestor, or I receive an email from a cousin, I slip a quick note into my file, where I can find it later. I don't keep originals in these folders, but if you do, look into archival-quality file folders to preserve your precious materials.

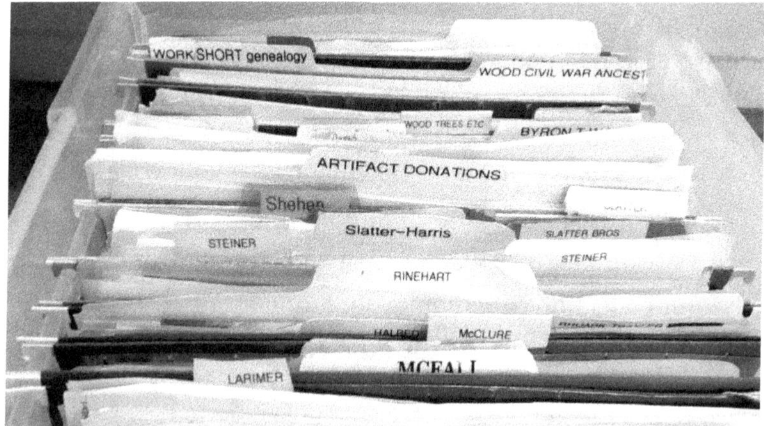


I also file printouts of Census pages, draft registration cards, and other documents (usually with my notes) inside surname file folders. This may seem like a lot of paper, but paper is sometimes more convenient than digital info. My paper-based files allow me to continue working on family history projects in the event of an online outage or a problem with digital files. I don't keep every piece of paper, but paper is often very useful for my purposes.

You can buy file folders in various colors if you want to organize by surnames, side of family, or another way of categorizing your paperwork. You also have the option of using labels in different colors to indicate side of family or surname, etc. However, in my experience, too many colors can be distracting and unproductive, especially if you're using a large number of folders and labels.

Follow your preference for how to file materials and arrange the files in folders for easy access. You can organize in various ways. Two common approaches are to file alphabetically by surname or by type of document. Another way is to organize by family group. As shown on the previous page, I group together folders for the intermarried families of Larimer, McFall, and McClure.

I like to physically separate the file folders into different file drawers according to side of the family. All surname/family folders for my mother's side are in one drawer, all surname/file folders for my father's side are in a different drawer.

Some people put hanging folders into tubs to store files that don't contain original documents, stacking the tubs inside closets or other out-of-the-way places. I use tubs for temporary storage of items I'm scanning and to hold files during short-term projects. In general, tubs aren't the best choice for long-term storage of originals.

## Binders

A second option is to organize in binders. You can choose binders in different sizes and colors to organize by surnames, side of family, etc. One genealogy friend has red binders for her side of the family and blue binders for her husband's side. She creates separate binders for each generation. Another genealogist has surname binders, plus separate binders for certain types of documents (military, birth, marriage, death).

Binders are handy when you want to tote documents on a research trip or show them to family members. Dressed up with a table of contents, with the spine and front of each binder clearly labelled, binders can help you tell a family's story through copies of paperwork and photos.

Never let your original documents near a hole-punch. Protect originals and good copies by slipping them into storage sleeves fitted for binders. The clear sleeve prevents tears and wrinkles without obscuring any part of the document, front or back. More about sleeves later.

You can use dividers and tabs to identify each section within a binder. The tabs help you find documents quickly,

and show at a glance what's inside. The photo above shows individual family pages separated by tabs within a surname binder. Notice that the tabs are adhered to the sleeves holding the documents, not to the documents themselves.

As with file folders, you can arrange your binders on the shelf alphabetically, by generation, by type of document, or a combination of all three. Consider using the color of the label as another cue to the contents of each binder.

## Boxes (sometimes tubs)

Plastic tubs (plastic tote containers) work for *temporary* storage, but not for long-term storage of photos, original documents, and other paper-based materials, say experts like the U.S. Library of Congress: www.loc.gov/preservation/about/faqs/photographs.html. If you're thinking about storing your collection in plastic tubs because you worry about water or insect damage, rethink where your materials are stored. Still, tubs are much better than nothing.

I'm a *big* fan of archival boxes for storing old photos (each in a separate sleeve), bulky items (my father's WWII memorabilia), and oversized items (my father-in-law's college scrapbook). If you have a family Bible or another specialized item, look for an archival box designed to keep it in good condition, now and into the future.

I use acid-free archival boxes with metal-reinforced corners so I can stack them without worrying that the boxes will collapse. These are available from a number of suppliers. You can ask for recommendations from your genealogy club, local or regional historical societies, public and college libraries, nearby museums, or browse groups online for recommendations.

Plan ahead before you buy: Estimate the size and volume of what will be in each box, shop around and compare, and buy a couple of boxes to try first. You'll want to keep families or surnames separate, avoid crowding items into boxes, and clearly label materials.

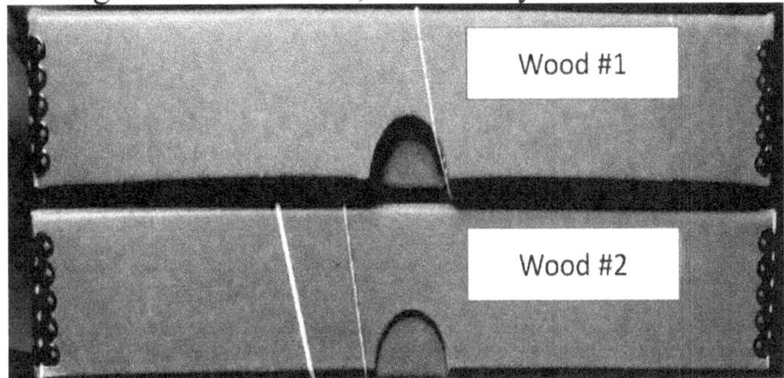


In all, I needed 30 archival boxes in various sizes to neatly store photos, photo albums, college memorabilia, and other items. These are easily accessible on shelves in my home office, neatly stacked, each with a label, ready to be passed to heirs when the time comes.

Read more about safe storage at the U.S. Library of Congress (www.loc.gov/preservation/care/index.html) and about preservation on this page from the U.S. National Archives (https://tinyurl.com/496s2yvu).

## Your trusty label maker

Plan on using a good label maker or plain adhesive labels to identify folders, binders, and boxes. Label makers can be as basic or as elaborate as your budget allows, and blank labels are inexpensive. Browse a nearby office-supply store or check online to view options. Don't forget to buy extra tape or labels, because you don't want to run out in the middle of organizing.

Using my favorite label maker, I mark each file folder and two sides of each storage box. You might want to use different label colors to denote different contents or surnames. Later in the organizing process, you'll be inventorying the contents of each box and tucking the inventory inside the corresponding box. So if you have multiple boxes for one family or surname, label them more specifically (Wood #1, Wood 1917 photo album, etc.) for clarity.

## Put a sleeve on it

Old photos and original documents are much safer inside clear, acid-free sleeves or envelopes than if they touch each other or are left rattling around loose in a file or box. I encourage you to make archival sleeves part of your plan. They're not expensive and the investment will allow you to protect your precious images for now and later, with future generations in mind.

Many companies offer clear, protective archival sleeves and envelopes made especially for photos or documents. You can do an online search, or ask a local museum/historical society for recommendations. If you're going to organize documents into binders, get clear sleeves that fit into binders.

I buy sleeves in two sizes: 5 x 7 inches and 11 x 14 inches, to accommodate smaller photos and larger certificates stacked in my archival boxes. Little by little, I'm slipping items into sleeves, sealing the sleeves, and sticking a label on the outside with bare-bones info jotted down. I still have a number of photos awaiting captioning, but at least they're safe in archival sleeves and organized inside my archival boxes. Read more about captioning in the next chapter.

## To sum up:

√ Do your homework before deciding on a method for organized storage, and see what professionals recommend.
√ Consider *files and folders, binders,* or *boxes (*sometimes *tubs).*
√ Ask genealogy friends or experts how they organize.
√ Label your files, boxes, and binders.
√ Put photos, original documents, and other materials into clear, acid-free sleeves or archival envelopes to keep them safe.
√ Add brief identifying info on the outside of each sleeve.

# CHAPTER 2
## ORGANIZE YOUR PHOTOS, IMAGES, AND MOVIES

Once you've thought about organized storage (files, binders, or boxes) for your collection, you'll need a strategy to sort, organize, label/caption, and store different kinds of photos, movies, and images. Whether you have century-old family portraits, a handful of Polaroids, an old scrapbook, home movies from the past, or a box filled with 35mm slides, this chapter will give you ideas for putting images in order—another element of Step 1 in the PASS process.

### Sorting photos and negatives

Sort photos with clean hands on a clean, dry surface away from food, drink, and anything with a strong aroma.

If you find notes attached to photos, remove clips and staples, but keep the photos and notes in order so you can analyze later. Also remove any rubber bands from photos and envelopes!

As you sort photos and

organize them (perhaps by surname, family, or date), winnow out fuzzy photos and others that are of low quality or not needed. Especially if you have better-quality photos taken at the same time, or with the same people or place, you may want to discard those of poor quality. Before discarding, consider whether technology will help you improve digitized copies of low-quality photos. You can even try to colorize copies if you choose.

**Caution:** If you want to experiment, be sure to *retain the original photo* and *original scan* as is. You should leave all originals in the best possible condition for future generations.

As you sort your photos, choose the best one among similar ones to keep for your collection. Consider giving extras or dupes to a relative (maybe a descendant of the person in the photo).

As a general rule, hold onto photos (and slides) with people and family homes or businesses, family cars, family pets, heirlooms, and other meaningful and recognizable images. You may not be able to identify everyone or everything now, but new information could become available in the future. Think about giving away or tossing the rest, if no one else in the family is interested.

But before you discard non-family photos and slides, do consider whether a historical society, archive, library, or museum might want a particular image or more than one for its collection.

If you have a photo or slide that might be from a hometown or somewhere else relevant to your family's history—but you don't know where—you can drop the digitized image into Google Images Search (https://images.google.com/) and see whether a similar image pops up in the result. For more ideas about analyzing and preserving photos, see this video from the Genealogy Center at the Allen County Public Library: https://youtu.be/MREG0y-11ho.

## Special considerations for negatives

If your collection includes negatives from a special occasion (a wedding, for instance) and you don't have those photos, consider having a contact sheet made from the negatives or select a few negatives to print. Even if the colors in color negatives have shifted over time, the images themselves may still be significant.

In the past, I went to a photo lab and had a contact sheet made from black-and-white negatives I didn't recognize. These days, I scan each negative at a high resolution (as shown here) and use photo software to invert the colors, turning black to white and white to black.

Then I digitally adjust the contrast and sharpen to see faces and details more clearly. I can enlarge and show to relatives, ask who's who, and digitally caption directly on a copy of the image (as shown on the enhanced image).

*Take care with storage:* After sorting, do not store negatives with photos, because the materials will interact and deteriorate. I learned the hard way that color negatives fade over time when stored with a mix of negatives and snapshots. So plan now to keep negatives away from photos. As noted earlier, if you choose to "colorize" or digitally restore faded images, preserve the originals intact.

For more, see this page on the U.S. Library of Congress website (www.loc.gov/preservation/care/photo.html), and two pages from the informative website of the U.S. National Archives (www.archives.gov/preservation/family-archives), and (https://tinyurl.com/4wv2h4ss).

Also check the Family Search site for additional details and recommendations about how to safely store old photos (https://tinyurl.com/432jtn2m). Finally, Cyndi's List has numerous links (www.cyndislist.com/photos/general/) to information about photo storage and names of specialized suppliers, but do ask genealogy friends and groups for recommendations.

## Caption photos to keep ancestors alive

My plan is to identify every photo, along with dates and places if possible, before I join my ancestors. Sometimes I know a lot about a photo, sometimes almost nothing. But if I can identify anyone or anything, the photo should have a caption to pass what I know to the next generation and beyond. This keeps ancestors alive for descendants, faces as well as information.

I use full names where possible so it's clear who's who in each photo, adding dates as well. This is particularly helpful when certain names appear in successive generations. Also, I try to identify people by relationship, such as: "Marian's paternal Grandpa Tivador Schaw," to clarify the family connection. If the photo simply says "Grandpa," will future generations know which grandpa?

Years ago, I inherited a mystery photo labeled "Mama" but no name or date, and no indication of whose mama she was. (She was a distant cousin's mama, I eventually learned, driving home the point that adding names, dates, and relationships are important when captioning old family photos.)

Ideally, captions should explain who's who and when/where/why each photo was taken. If a number of people appear in the picture, you can identify them using phrases like "Pictured, left to right," "Seated, left to right," or "Front row, left to right." Add relationship information if possible.

Mention any details you know while they're fresh in your mind: place, date, occasion, whatever is relevant. Future generations may not have anyone to ask about these photos, so write down at least the basics. If you decide to share these images with relatives, you also want to share what you know about these ancestors.

## Write captions on paper or labels

It's tempting, but *not* a good idea to mark on your original photos or documents, even if you use special pens or pencils that are supposed to be safe. Instead, write on labels or pieces of paper you can place on the outside of your clear sleeves or envelopes. Labels don't have to be fancy, just informative and clearly written. Also "caption" slides and movies after you've sorted them.

If you write a long caption, tape a piece of paper with your notations to the outside of the sleeve or envelope. Your original stays safe, no markings or clips, staples, or rubber bands to damage the photo, and the detailed info stays with it. Just tape the page to the outside of the sleeve and it will stay with the photo.

Short captions can be printed or handwritten on adhesive labels and placed on the outside of sleeves. For example, in the 1920s photo shown here, an ancestor is sitting on a pony that a promoter brought around to apartment houses in New York City, as a photo opportunity.

Relatives and descendants might find it interesting to know why a pony was on a Manhattan sidewalk! To share the story, I hand-printed my caption on a label and put it on the front of the clear sleeve holding the original photo.

In a few cases, I typed a longer explanation of a photo (such as a reunion photo where I was a youngster standing with the extended family). Then I added a digital version of the photo to the typed page of notes, printed it, and attached it to the photo's envelope. I also put a copy in the surname or family file. Putting information in more than one place serves as informal backup.

## Downsize and sort slides

Without question, 35mm and other size slide transparencies represent *old* technology. How many of our descendants will have or want a slide projector? I have one spare projector bulb. In 10 or 20 years, will another bulb be available if descendants want to view slides? Probably not. Will they even know what a projector was? So it's time to sort slides, salvage the meaningful ones, convert them to newer technology, and caption the images.

My late father-in-law left a dozen slide trays filled mainly with travel images and the occasional family photo. If those little faces don't escape from these old slides, interesting family 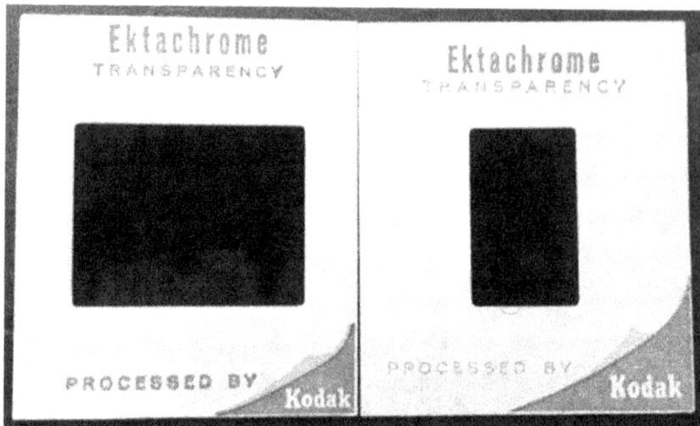



stories may not come to light. Some of my big breakthroughs have come when a cousin recognized a face and recalled a family story.

That's why I made it a priority to sort the slides and get the meaningful ones into shape for the next generation. After sorting, I stored some of the key slides in archival clear sleeves and grouped others in slide boxes, marked with names/dates.

With apologies to my dad-in-law, 95% of his slides were of well-known world landmarks, trees and flowers, roadside scenes, and sightseeing scenes; not of interest to the next generation, not of value for family history. No relatives wanted these slides, so I tossed them. I saved the relative handful of slides with people and recognizable family homes, backyards, rooms, cars, or party scenes.

If you're not sure whether a particular slide is significant for family history, ask a relative's opinion. If you decide to part with a slide or photo showing a local scene from the past, find out whether a museum or other institution would be interested. Maybe the slide is from a period when few local images survived, or the image features long-gone buildings, local luminaries from the past, etc. You can try to find it a good new home, not in your collection.

## Scan your slides

For detailed instructions about how to scan slides, do an online search for "scanning slides." You'll find there are numerous options, including apps, devices, and services. Also check whether a nearby library or Family History Center has scanning equipment. Some invite the public to use their equipment without charge. Call and check!

If you don't want to scan slides yourself, you can go to a store or service that will dust them, scan at high resolution, and provide digital images. To find vendors, look at sites such as Cyndi's List (www.cyndislist.com/scanners/vendors), and shop around. The cost per slide isn't much but it adds up if you scan many slides.

For the most precious, one-of-a-kind family slides, I believe that using a service is worth the extra money. I chose the most important family slides from my father-in-law's collection and paid for a service to clean and digitize them.

For other slides, I used my home scanners to digitize those I believed were worth saving—recognizable people, places, and occasions, mainly. When I could put a name to the face, I filed the image digitally by surname. Now the images are no longer trapped on tiny slides but can be printed as photos and distributed to family members, digitally or in print.

Organize and store the original slides in archival sleeves or other safe containers, away from heat and moisture. They've survived this long and you want them to be available to your family in the future.

## Caption and share digitized images

Write the captions (digitally or on labels) now while you and your relatives can remember something about these images. Consider carefully whether to post digitized, captioned images on any online family tree. *Important:* Understand the terms of service of a tree site or genealogy site before you post any images or other content of your own. In any case, avoid public posting of photos showing living people, and don't publicly use their names in captions without permission.

Hubby and I sent prints of digitized slides to Wood relatives for help in figuring out who was who. It was fun to enlarge a couple of slides of holidays in his childhood home, which would never have been seen again if they were still in outdated slide technology. The family welcomed the opportunity to talk about these old images, which in turn allowed me to capture a new story.

Whether you currently use USB flash drives, an external hard drive, or the cloud to store your scans, keep an eye on the latest technology and be ready to switch to newer media or methods as needed. Remember, you're not just organizing for yourself. You want the next generation and beyond to be able to access these images. Don't wait to upgrade your storage until the tech is outdated. Back up everything, just in case, as I discuss later in the book.

## Save your movies

For old family movies, whether Super 8, VHS, or any other outdated format, arrange to transfer the content to a newer technology as soon as possible. Older media deteriorate year by year. You don't want to lose movies or videos of weddings, graduations, or holiday times.

In the past, to save the family history content of VHS tapes, I paid a well-known store to do the transfer to high-quality DVDs with access to downloadable digital content. The result: cleaned-up versions that are viewable and upgradable to newer media. These days, many services will turn your old movies or tapes into digital video content accessed via cloud storage.

If you use DVDs or similar media, the U.S. National Archives suggests backing up with a good quality "storage" copy of the movie, one that you won't actually use very often (see https://tinyurl.com/rbchuscs). Carefully label the new media so you won't lose track of what you have, where it's stored, who's in each movie, the date, and other details.

A cousin had a more sophisticated, more costly solution to organizing a box of Super 8 reels from the 1930s to the 1950s. He had a studio professionally transfer specific parts of the movies (such as from a family wedding and a family picnic) onto a master DVD, arranging them in chronological order.

The originals had no sound, so my cousin wrote title cards to be shown for a few seconds before each section. Another cousin kindly narrated the DVD for me, while I taped her and made notes. I can now do screen captures and label each person for future generations.

(It was poignant to see my mother as a teenager at the beach, by the way!) Of course, I am digitizing this DVD so it I can access it via newer technology.

## To sum up:

√ Sort, separate, and analyze photos, negatives, and slides.
√ Research safe storage for photos, negatives, and slides.
√ Have contact sheets made from negatives OR scan negatives, invert to turn dark into light, and sharpen to see details.
√ Store negatives *away* from photos.
√ Caption all images, adding as much detail as you know.
√ Write captions on paper or labels, *not* directly on originals; consider digitally captioning directly on copies of images.
√ Avoid public posting of photos showing or captioning living people.
√ Save movies by updating to new technology, more than once if needed before old technology is obsolete.
√ Store all originals and digital images safely, with backup for everything you've digitized.

# CHAPTER 3
## ORGANIZING DIGITAL FILES AND EMAILS

You know all those original documents, photos, and slides you just sorted and organized into folders or binders or boxes? Over time, it would be a good idea to digitize them and store them electronically. *Life by the inch is a cinch.* Digitizing is a "by the inch" activity.

## Why digitize?

Old paper and photos can be fragile and deteriorate over the years. Even when you use the best storage options for printed photos and documents, you don't want to handle originals very often. Digitizing means your genealogy materials will be available and looking good for years to come, without harming the originals.

You can magnify any part of the digital image on your computer screen to get a close look (at a face, a postmark, or a signature, for example). With technology, you can change colors, darken pen or pencil marks, repair tears, and tease more clues out of what you digitize, to solve family-history mysteries.

Of course, you'll want to hold onto most of the originals, even after you digitize. But by going digital, you have more options for sharing. Anything you've scanned can be shared electronically among family members and possibly posted on genealogy websites (keep privacy and copyright in mind). You'll also have more options for investigating and documenting your family's past by analyzing digitized materials and captioning them.

If you digitize your collection little by little, you'll eventually get it done—and your heirs will thank you. No deadlines, no pressure, just digitize when you have a few minutes. Choose a box or folder and mark your place if you stop, so you can return to digitizing until you complete that unit. Finished digitizing a box or file? Mark it (on a list or on the label) as a reminder that you can move on. Then keep going, one file or box or album at a time.

In the past, when I digitized an album, I prepared a DVD and sent it to family members, along with a note about the background of the photos (where/when). They were delighted to get this surprise in the mail, and I was glad to share the faces and stories from the past. As technology changed, I mailed USB flash drives. These days, I'm sharing digitized files electronically and via the cloud.

## Not entirely paperless genealogy

Consider retaining paper items (and printing key digital items) for one big reason: Technology changes, and properly-stored physical materials (photos, documents) are likely to be accessible in decades, whereas digital items stored on yesterday's or today's media may not be. This is the informed view of tech guru Vinton Cerf, speaking to the American Association for the Advancement of Science.

If you have family photos on your phone, tablet, or social-media sites, remember to download regularly and file electronically. Think about printing the best or most significant, whether you plan to share now or frame or file with your physical materials.

Going entirely paperless is not necessarily your goal at this point. What you want to do is make family history accessible to the next generation and beyond. If you have no immediate heirs, you may find places to donate paper (and possibly digital) items from your collection. Printing your digital-only materials is a small measure of protection and also gives you something to file for easy availability when you are doing research.

## Sources for digitizing

Seek out recommendations for apps, scanners, scanning techniques, services, and other alternatives on authoritative sites. The U.S.

Library of Congress offers a variety of ideas on its site (see page at https://tinyurl.com/ca84f6s4). On Facebook, look at Technology for Genealogy (www.facebook.com/groups/techgen/). Also check other social media pages and discussions, or ask a local library for ideas about how to digitize. Rather than go into specifics here, I defer to experts with the latest information.

My key piece of advice is this: *Scan at a high resolution.* You don't want to go back and rescan later because your image lacks the detail you need to magnify it or make a quality print. I thought I was saving storage space by scanning items at a fairly low resolution. Not smart. I had to rescan items when more detail was needed.

Today, the storage capacity of hard drives and cloud services is so vast that you can store many high-resolution items at a low cost. So don't stint on the resolution. Scan at the highest resolution you can and you won't have to redo your work.

## File your digital files and emails

To make life easy, organize your digital images, digitized documents, and email messages into electronic folders that mirror or are similar to your filing system for physical items. Be sure your electronic folder and file names are descriptive so you can tell at a glance what's in each file.

> ▾ Freeland family
>    Earle Larimer Freeland1918draft
>    EarleFreelandDeath1943
>    EarleLarimerFreelandDeathCertP1.jpg
>    EarleLarimerFreelandDeathCertP2.jpg
>    Freeland_Earl_ETobit_22Jan1920.pdf
>    Freeland_Emma_ ETobit_19 Sept1923.pdf
>    Freeland_Family_index.docx
>    Freeland_James_ ETobit_16 Sept1920.pdf
>    Freeland_James_C_ ETobit1_ 31 Dec2005.pdf
>    LucyRFreelandArtist1917_Directory.png
>    Ringer_Flora_ Freeland_obit_10 Aug1960.pdf

I like to have a matching physical file in my file drawer, so I can put my hands on info in a hurry. If you keep all military records in one binder or file, for instance, you may want to file digital versions in the same way (plus put a digital copy into each surname or family folder, just in case). The best method is one that works for *you*.

The illustration on the previous page is from one of my digital family folders. I've put all scanned documents, photos, and news clippings into this folder for a particular family. When I began, my file names were less specific than they are now, and I recommend that you use even more detailed file names than in my illustration. Slowly, I'm renaming and refiling digital items. My emails about this family are filed similarly on my computer.

Consider what other methods might work well for your personal situation. Devon Lee of Family History Fanatics likes a method she shows in more detail in her informative video (at www.youtube.com/watch?v=dfR7ivYASyY).

Some of my genealogy friends rely on tech like Evernote (https://evernote.com/) and Trello (https://trello.com) to store data they need. Others prefer spreadsheets or use different technology, depending on their specific needs.

If this is your cup of cocoa, do an online search for good sources and expert advice to get started. Friends who use such software say it saves time after the initial learning curve. Plus, they can downsize their written notes after filing electronically, and still find what they want quickly.

## Digitize captions

As you digitize your photos, consider adding digital captions to a copy of the digitized image. I like using my photo software to superimpose names near faces. Then I can print and share with family, and file digitally.

This example shows only given names, but you can easily add surnames and more information. Yes, I have written captions on the

outside of the sleeves of these photos. But I also want to include the captions on copies of the digital versions.

Especially when I share with relatives, having names and details

on a *copy* of the image can keep these ancestors alive in multiple lines of my family. I now add digital captions and source info to family photos I upload to genealogy sites, after understanding how the site is legally allowed to use my content.

Note that I went beyond name to mention the family as source. The caption was excellent cousin bait, as well as a not-so-subtle reminder of attribution!

If you share, please be mindful of not invading the privacy of living people. Unless you have permission from a relative, don't label that person or publicly post a photo of that person.

Also, remember to respect the rules of copyight for photos you or your family haven't personally snapped.

## Back up regularly

Don't risk losing your valuable files if your computer or hard drive loses its mind! Back up regularly, both digitized documents and images and possibly email, and be ready for the worst-case scenario. Just in case, consider having more than one method of backing up your genealogy files.

Get specifics about how, where, and when to back up your digital files from sources such as the Technology for Genealogy page on Facebook (www.facebook.com/groups/techgen) and Brigham Young University's Family History Library YouTube channel (www.youtube.com/c/BYUFamilyHistoryLibrary/videos), among many other sources.

I back up my digital work on an external hard drive and in the cloud, but you can use a flash drive for temporary storage, or possibly network attached storage, or some combination. In fact, use more than one backup method, such as automated backup to off-site cloud storage, as well as to your own external drive every day. I know from personal experience the aggravation of losing digital files, so I back up.

Paper copies are an easy backup plan for the most vital items. I make paper copies from key originals that I've digitized, and file the copies in family or surname folders and boxes.

Your genealogy heirs may not be familiar with the technology you use, so printed copies of key documents and photos makes things very simple for those who come after us.

## To sum up:

√   Digitize documents and photos at high resolution to preserve them, be able to magnify, and use other tricks to find clues.

√   Research digitization and electronic storage options, and keep up as technology changes.

√   File digitized documents and emails in a way that's similar to how you organize your paper materials.

√   Digitize captions along with images to keep ancestors alive and indicate the source of these images.

√   Before uploading photos to genealogy sites, understand how each site is legally allowed to use your content.

√   Consider printing key documents for your paper files.

√   Back up regularly, preferably using multiple methods!

# CHAPTER 4
## INVENTORY AND INDEX YOUR COLLECTION

By inventorying each of your boxes, binders, or folders as part of Step 1 in the four-step PASS process, you and your heirs (relatives and/or institutions) will get a clearer picture of:

- What physical items (photos, documents, etc.) are in your collection;
- Where, exactly, each physical item is located;
- How each physical item relates to your family tree; and, just as important . . .
- Which documents or other items you don't have in your collection.

**Why inventory?**

Putting an inventory list in each box or each binder/folder will help you or your heirs locate items easily, without taking everything out to look. I also put copies of the inventory into the folders/binders of family members who are mentioned in the contents list. Yet another benefit is that as you inventory, you get a mental picture of how different items tell the story of your ancestors. You might have a new insight to solve a genealogy mystery after comparing photos in different boxes or discovering that letters in different folders were postmarked on the same day. Clues often turn up during inventory.

Or, like me, maybe you'll realize that you should have a document—like naturalization paperwork—but you don't! (Keep a list and do the research later—try not to get sidetracked now.)

To avoid getting overwhelmed, work on the inventory for one box or one binder at a time, whenever you can spare an hour (life by the inch). Then slip a piece of paper between items to mark your place when you stop. You can go back when you have more time to take inventory. Before long, you'll have one inventory completed and be ready to move on to the next. And the next.

## How to take inventory

Below is a sample inventory for an archival box of materials related to my grandfather. I'm going to describe the process I used. It's not difficult, but inventorying does take a little time.

### Sample Inventory

Contents of Schaw #1 Box
(Tivador Schaw was Marian's paternal grandpa)
Inventoried on June 1, 2021 by Marian Wood

| Item | Date | Place | Comments |
|---|---|---|---|
| Schaw siblings photo (size about 5" x 7"). Three sisters in fancy dress, one brother in Hungarian military uniform | 1915, June 3<br><br>Handwritten date on front | Ungvar, Hungary (now Uzhhorod, Ukraine) | Sepia, with handwritten inscription on reverse: "For dear Tivador" |
| Schaw, Tivador - U.S. naturalization certificate #214 | 1911, May 9<br><br>Date stamp | New York, New York, U.S.A. | Tivador was 24 years old, living at 282 Avenue C, New York City |

Spread items from one box or folder on a clean, dry surface, and examine them, one by one. Your goal is to describe each item succinctly, explain its significance, and put it into a genealogical context. You want anyone who opens the folder or box to be able to match the item to the description, as shown in this sample inventory.

My personal preference is to rule columns on a legal pad and do a first draft by hand as I pick up each item. Later, I'll enter the information on my computer. This way, I can leave the handwritten list in the box or binder when I break off for the day, and keep going without having my computer next to me. However, you might prefer to use your tablet or laptop for this purpose, rather than writing by hand. Make columns sortable and entries searchable for easy access.

When I have more than one box or folder for a particular surname or family, I label the box and the inventory page "Schaw #1" or "Burk photos #1" to indicate which box is being inventoried. Use your own label method, not necessarily mine.

As you inventory, try adding extra information. For example, if you have multiple photos of a particular family, describe each by size as well as by occasion, etc. If possible, write a bit about the context, such as inscriptions, postmarks, places, and other details. Another reason I add detail is that I haven't yet captioned every photo, so the inventory gives me an opportunity to share something about each item with my heirs.

When you transcribe your notes into a spreadsheet or word-processed document or database file, create columns with headings. You want to be able to sort by date or place, for instance. Here, I've entered dates with year first, so I can sort easily and find what I'm looking for—and notice clues later, after finishing the inventory.

Include a title at the top of each inventory sheet (naming the box or file or binder where it will be placed), add your name, and include the date of your inventory. Change the date when you add more items to the binder or box. For the sake of genealogy heirs who aren't familiar with everyone in the family tree, you may want to explain how this surname or family is related to you, as shown in my sample.

Putting your materials in order and taking inventory is an accomplishment! It also gets you ready for indexing. An index shows where an ancestor is mentioned in the collection—a vital link between your research and your analysis.

## Get ready to index

Whether your collection includes a small bundle of letters, a decade's worth of diaries, or a baby book listing gifts and visitors, you'll learn a lot by indexing. Here is a sample index similar to one I did for a set of diaries.

### Sample Index
### Index to Mac McClure diaries
### Updated by Marian Wood
### on May 12, 2021

Mac McClure, great uncle of Marian Wood, was the older son of Janice Brown McClure and Alexander McClure. Mac kept diaries from 1959-1986 (now stored in Marian's home office).

| *Name* | *Relationship* | *Date* | *Place* | *Comments* |
|---|---|---|---|---|
| Brown, William (Billy) | Mac's first cousin on his mother's side. | 1964, Nov. 27 | Indiana, Wabash | Quote: "Drove to Wabash, Indiana, for Thanksgiving dinner with Billy. He showed slides of the Brown reunion." |
| Surname, given (nickname or maiden name) | Relationship | Year first | State or country first | Note any extra info |

The top four reasons to index:

**1.** Your relatives and heirs will be able to look up family members by name (or check a date) and turn to the proper page or section of the documents for that entry.

**2.** You can clarify discrepancies by comparing information in informal family documents with official government records and other formal documents.

**3.** You can follow individuals through the years by tracing their movements via the documents, revealing changes or relationships not obvious without the index.

**4.** By comparing the index of multiple records, you may uncover clues to identify mystery photos or to discover new family ties.

Consider indexing anything that might include the names of your ancestors' friends, associates, and neighbors (the FAN club). For example, you can index the names in items like family diaries and letters, scrapbooks, photo and wedding albums, baby books, family society minutes, funeral sign-in sheets, probate documents, oral histories, and on and on.

Indexing is an inch-by-inch process. Just note where you stop so you can return to the right spot when you resume indexing.

## Plan your index format

My computer-based indexes include five columns, as shown in the sample. Set up columns depending on what you're indexing and what you want to record or identify. The point of multiple columns is to be able to *digitally sort* each column when you wish to locate a person or correlate documents. And of course digitally search too.

As with inventorying, I prefer to handwrite the first draft, but use the method that works for you. I rule a legal pad into columns and take notes by hand. If you prefer to take inventory directly on your laptop or tablet, just create a table on the screen or use a spreadsheet or database. Enter your notes as you handle each item. Mine the data in each item so your index is robust.

Whether you're using paper or a computer, head the index page with a title to describe the document(s) you are indexing. Include dates if possible. For example: Index to John Doe's diaries, 1950-1960 or Index to Sadie Sample's baby book, 1930. Add your name and the date (at least month and year) to your index.

As a starting point, you can note the following in your index:

- *Name of each person mentioned* (list surname first—you can alphabetize and sort later).
- *Relationship* (be as specific as possible; identify "guesses").
- *Date* (including year, month, day—allowing you to sort chronologically if you choose)

- *Place* (be specific and consistent, either naming country first or city/town and state/province, or state/province and city).
- *Comments* (details, context, significance; refer to other documents if necessary; explain who's who and why people might be mentioned or *not* mentioned).

Place a copy of the index with the item(s) you indexed and put copies inside surname files. I have four pages of index entries tucked into the box with my ancestor's diaries. Anyone can see at a glance what the contents are and how the people in the diary entries relate to the family as a whole. While some relatives can still remember these people or events, I want to note the details in my index for future generations to appreciate. I also update the index when I learn something that explains an entry in the diaries.

## Six easy steps to indexing

Let me share six step-by-step instructions for easy indexing.

*1. Put items in chronological order.* Put all diaries or letters or programs in order, earliest to latest. That way, you'll be able to follow along as the narrative mentions upcoming events or evolving relationships. I did this with letters written to my mother during the time she first met and began dating my father. It was exciting to read what led up to his proposal and their future plans! And I could understand later letters based on the context of earlier letters.

*2. Focus on one item at a time.* Pick up one letter, one month of the diary, one of anything in your collection and start to index. If you feel like doing more, go for it. Give yourself a pat on the back every time you index an entire box or folder! If you have the time to continue, index until you run out of steam for the day.

*3. Identify the people and their relationships.* The first time you see a name mentioned, write it down in full (with nicknames if it helps jog memories). Note the relationship to your family, if you know it. Also jot down the date or some other way of going back to that document for the full reference. If you see a name mentioned repeatedly, note it even if you don't know the relationship. As you continue to index, watch for clues to that person's relationship with the family. Later, you can alphabetize the list of people (sorting by surname). For now, just make notes, including notes to ask relatives for any relevant details.

*4. Compile your list of people, dates, and brief explanations.* For instance, I identified Brown, William ("Billy") by full name and nickname in my index. I also noted how Billy was related to the person who wrote the diaries, Mac McClure. In "comments," I indicated the substance of this entry.

*5. Type your index, listing people alphabetically by surname.* You can sort all columns later if you do this in a spreadsheet or a digital document. Your index is a handy reference when you're researching an ancestor, and it will be of help to people in the future. Update your index as you learn more about the relationships.

*6. Talk up your index!* Tell relatives what you've learned, and offer them copies of the index and relevant sections of the items indexed. Who doesn't want to know something new about a parent or grandparent, whether a hint of personality or an anecdote?

## After indexing, look for clues

Before you file your index, search it for clues to family relationships and mysteries. You're not indexing simply for the sake of getting organized—the process is important for making progress on your research right now. My indexing has helped me solve family mysteries, and you might have similar success!

Here are some ways you can use an index to deepen your knowledge of family history:

*Watch for groups of people and repeat appearances.* Sometimes a letter or diary mention of several people getting together is actually about a family occasion. If certain names pop up regularly, especially on significant dates (such as a birthday or a holiday), chances are they are connected to your family. It won't take long to determine which people you should be following closely and which people seem to be just casual friends. Maybe you can even match the mentions to photos in your collection.

*Watch for disappearances and enigmatic mentions.* Sometimes people are mentioned only once--did they move away, was there a quarrel, did they pass away, was there a divorce? This is the puzzle part of genealogy research. Another relative might have insight if you discuss what you found out and ask about the mysteries.

*Check dates against what you know.* Does the index help you narrow down possible birth, marriage, death dates? Does it fill in the blanks on where ancestors were during key periods? Who is missing on key dates? During indexing, I noticed that a great aunt was suddenly absent from family tree meetings. That was a clue to a possible death date, which I'd been unable to pinpoint—until I indexed notes taken at these meetings.

*Look at relationships.* Does the index shed light on whether family members were estranged or close? Does it confirm relationships you suspected? Who is present at family gatherings, and how often do they show up? One set of family meeting minutes showed how warmly a widowed in-law was welcomed, along with her second family. As I indexed, I noticed the rare attendance of an uncle whose marriage outside the faith was frowned upon.

*Look at occasions.* Who's visiting on holidays? Which holidays are celebrated? Are weddings, birthdays, funerals mentioned? Who's giving gifts, who's receiving gifts? One baby book I indexed gave me a clue that someone was more than a "family friend" because she gave a really valuable gift. Sure enough, once I dug a lot deeper, she turned out to be the ex-wife of a close relative.

*Cross-reference the index against other items.* Do you have photos of the people mentioned in the index during the period covered by the documents? See whether the index can help you identify mystery faces or give you more context for when, where, and why the photos were taken. Dates can be so useful in an index.

*Confirm details to verify.* If a diary mentions someone's birth, marriage, or death, compare the dates with official documents. A century ago, official records weren't always filed on time, so a birth date on the vital records form might be earlier or later than the actual birth. Maybe the index will point you in the right direction.

The spelling of names on Census forms wasn't always accurate, so check your index against the Census. Use the index to match nicknames with full given names on your tree. You might find a variation via the index that you can use to search creatively for that person. If so, note it so you can use it in your future research.

## Solving family-history mysteries

Here's how indexing helped me solve another genealogical mystery.

My sister-in-law remembered a cousin Edith, quite a tall lady, attending her wedding years ago. Now no one could remember Edith's last name or how she was related to the family.

When I indexed my late father-in-law's diaries, I noted repeated mentions of "Edith" in the 1960s and 1970s, including one entry that referred to her as a cousin. This entry led my husband to a hunch about how Edith was actually related to his parents. Together with my sister-in-law's memories and some confirming Census data, we soon put Edith into position on the family tree as my father-in-law's first cousin. Knowing the dates and approximate ages also helped us tentatively identify this tall cousin in a photo with my father-in-law.

Without the diary index, would we have solved this mystery? I don't know, but the clues helped. If later research clarifies an ancestor's situation or solves a mystery, you may want to add notes to your index (and to your files) to explain further.

**To sum up:**

√ Inventory your genealogy materials to show what you have, what you *don't* have, and where items are stored.

√ Inventory one box or folder at a time, describing each item succinctly but in enough detail to identify it in context.

√ Index so you can quickly look up family members by name, trace individuals through the years, and discover clues to solve genealogical mysteries.

√ Make indexes sortable by column so you can alphabetize by surname or put in chronological order if desired.

√ To index, put items in chronological order, focus on one item at a time, identify who's who and how they're related, list people by surname, store the index with the materials.

√ Use indexes to find clues to ancestors and relationships.

√ Update your index if you later learn more that clarifies the context or meaning of an item, person, or place.

# CHAPTER 5
## RECORD YOUR FAMILY TREE

If only our ancestors had left us a neat, complete, fully-sourced family tree! Most of us began with just clues or scraps of a tree. We can preserve what we've learned over the years by writing it down in a pedigree chart, a family group sheet, or a family tree (or another format). This is a key part of Step 1 in the PASS process.

Recording names, dates, and places not only anchors each ancestor's position in the family tree, it also reveals gaps and serves as a reminder of future research needed. Plus, a chart or tree in every surname file, folder, binder, or box will help the genealogists of the next generation.

If you're thinking about leaving your collection to an institution, a family tree in some form will help non-family eyes understand who's who. In this case, a standardized format will help curators, archivists, and other professionals understand the family's past.

### Family group sheets and pedigree charts

Relatives who know little of a family's history may not be able to absorb all the names and relationships on a full family tree. I always invite relatives to view my online trees, but sometimes they find the number of people and the interconnections confusing. That's why I create pedigree charts and family group sheets, each focusing attention on a particular section of the overall family tree.

When a relative shows interest, I pull out a family group sheet and point to a particular person, mention the siblings, indicate the mother's maiden name, and tell a story if I know one connected to that branch of the family. (Also I show photos, to associate a face with a name wherever possible.)

Family group sheets provide room for including siblings and spouses of people in my direct line, a plus. You never know what you'll discover by tracing in-laws, sisters, or brothers! For example, documents from my grandpa's siblings helped me identify the family's home town. I went on to research children of the siblings and connected with cousins who knew more about our ancestry.

Pedigree charts are a great way to document the direct line of a mother's or father's tree. I used them to record how a branch of my husband's family descends from a Mayflower passenger. I sometimes carry charts for reference while doing genealogy research away from home. Like family group sheets, pedigree charts reveal at a glance whether I'm missing key people, places, or dates.

If you're using genealogy software, you can print family group sheets and pedigree charts with a tap or a click. Test your software's capabilities, but also look at other options. You may discover you prefer a different layout. My family likes more basic pedigree charts and family tree templates, which I download from free sources. I've also created my own handwritten and software-generated family trees—and, in the process, noted gaps for future research.

## Downloadable templates

A number of sites offer free download of templates for family group sheets, family trees, and pedigree charts. Do an online search (for terms like *downloadable pedigree chart*) or check these sources:

- Family Search (https://tinyurl.com/y42xmudf)

- Misbach Enterprises (www.misbach.org/)

- Cyndi's List (https://tinyurl.com/4d2k2e8b)


You can type directly on some of these charts (or hand write on a template you download and print, if you like). If you're doing the charts electronically, save your work with a descriptive file name and file the digital version. It's easy to make revisions when you discover new details. Date your forms and print more than one copy.

I try to file my electronic and printed pedigree charts in the corresponding surname files and boxes. I also put another copy in a file with other pedigrees/trees/family group sheets. Finally, I give updated printouts of the charts to cousins who are researching along with me, and to the genealogists of the next generation.

If you are considering donating your genealogy collection to an institution (see Chapter 10), try to guide curators and researchers through your materials by providing a written record. Your collection will ultimately be used to further research, which is why an understanding of the ancestral relationships is so important.

## Family trees: online, software, apps

If you don't have a family tree posted online, I encourage you to consider putting one up (not necessarily with documents or photos attached). Not only will you then be able to share with family members by giving them access, you'll also know that the tree will be available in the future. You have lots of choices of where to post a tree for free, such as the Family Search website (www.familysearch.org), the Ancestry website (www.ancestry.com), My Heritage (www.myheritage.com), Geni (www.geni.com), and the WikiTree website, (www.wikitree.com), to name a few popular genealogy sites.

My trees are public because I want cousins and distant relations to find me by finding mutual ancestors on trees. I've made numerous cousin connections through online trees (cousin bait!).

On some sites, you have the option to make a tree private, visible only to people you invite, if you wish. Even then, you can sometimes make a private tree searchable, allowing people to contact you if they have questions or information.

You can also not name living people on a tree, if privacy is a major concern. On some sites, living people are only visible to the tree creator (you) or someone who has your permission to view living people. Do your homework before you decide whether and how to post a tree, and whether to post photos and other content.

As a backup to my other records, I've occasionally taken screen shots of my online trees, family group by family group, and inserted these pages into my files and boxes. The family tree looks great on the screen, so it'll look just as good in a printout I give to relatives who don't use computers or who don't want to learn how to navigate an online tree.

I'm sold on genealogy software. It's easy to print out various reports and charts, and to export family trees (in Gedcom or other format) to exchange with relatives. If I want to print a report of relatives by home address (for a genealogy field trip), I can do that with a few clicks. My chosen software not only allows for backups, it syncs my online trees with trees kept on my home computer, another major advantage. This allows me to retain control of my tree, no matter what happens to the online trees in the future.

It's the age of apps, so also investigate how you can use your smartphone or tablet computer to further your genealogical research and have your tree and family history details at your fingertips. Some software and some genealogy websites offer apps for phone or tablet, allowing you to research and record family tree info from anywhere.

To learn more about genealogy software, check online sources such as Cyndi's List (www.cyndislist.com/software/), the popular Facebook Technology for Genealogy page (www.facebook.com/groups/techgen/), and Wikipedia (https://tinyurl.com/sh46pe7u), among other sites. You can check tech websites that review genealogy software and ask friends what they use, as well. If a software firm offers a trial period, try before you buy.


## To sum up:

√   Sometimes family group sheets and pedigree charts are easier to understand than a full family tree.

√   Give family group sheets, pedigree charts, and trees to relatives and to genealogists of the next generation.

√    One option is to download free templates from online sources.

√    Another option is to use genealogy software to record trees.

√    Consider posting family trees online and sharing with relatives. Cousin bait! But you may not want to share family photos on these sites.

√    Look into apps and software for convenient genealogy research, documenting trees, and other functions.

√    Remember to back up your work regularly.

# CHAPTER 6
## FAMILY ARTIFACTS: KEEP OR GIVE AWAY?

In Step 2 of the PASS process, you'll be making decisions about the items in your collection by curating what you have. You may not have room for every item, you may have duplicate items, or you may have items that don't even connect with your immediate family.

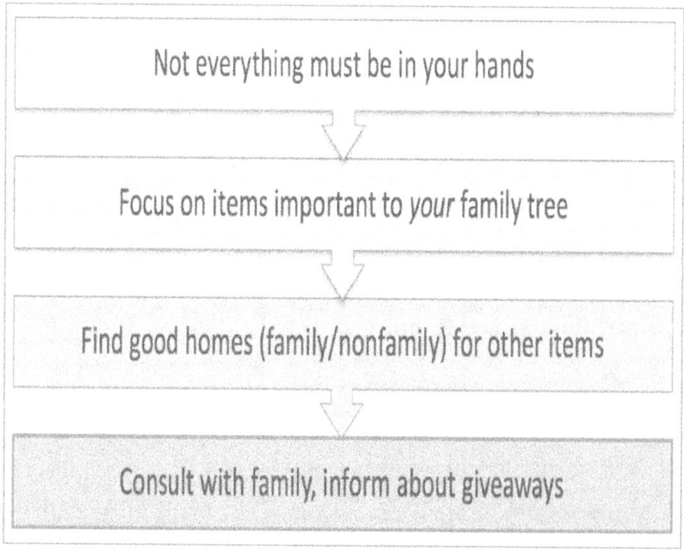


The key thing to remember is that *not everything* must be in your hands. Ideally, you'll focus on items most important to your family tree and think about good homes for other items—consulting with family, of course, before making final decisions about allocating ownership. Your objective is keep the artifacts safe, either in your hands or in the hands of others who have an interest in them.

Include family members in your curating decisions, especially if you're thinking about downsizing valuable items. Relatives may have strong opinions about particular items—so I encourage you to have a discussion before you take action. Chapter 7 discusses how to place items outside the family.

As you sort, spend a few minutes with each item, think about its meaning relative to your family's history, and consider its future.

## Keep or Give Away?

Sort items from your collection into three categories.

- Category 1: Items you really want to *keep* in your collection or *keep* in the hands of immediate family.
- Category 2: Items you want to *keep* in the extended family.
- Category 3: Items you want to *give away* to a good home outside the family (sell, donate, or otherwise distribute).

## Category 1: Keep (yourself or in the family)

The priority for category 1 is safeguarding the following types of items for future generations: (1) items related to your immediate family, (2) items related to your direct line, and (3) items from ancestors without descendants.

Items such as your parents' wedding album would be important to maintain in your own collection or in the hands of your siblings or children, for instance. So the significance won't be lost, identify these items and their role in the family, keep them well organized, and store safely to pass to the next generation. Ideally, items from your direct line (from your grandparents, great-grandparents, and so on) should also remain with your collection or within your immediate family, if possible.

If you inherited items from ancestors who had no descendants, classify them either with this category or with category 2. Take time to think about how you can best keep alive the memory of these ancestors and the artifacts they treasured. More about this topic later in the chapter.

## Category 1 example: One item, multiple heirs

Let's say you have your parents' wedding album, to be inherited in the future by one designated family heir. But if there are multiple heirs, why wait to share that item?

Consider turning the wedding album into a small photo book for descendants. I scanned all the photos from my parents' album at high resolution, uploaded the photos to a commercial photo book site, arranged them in order, and added captions to identify the folks in every photo (name and relationship). I also included some details of my parents' courtship and honeymoon, so future generations would know more about my parents' life together.

By printing these books, I not only shared a coveted item with everyone who wanted it, but also preserved the original intact and kept the stories alive for the next generation. The books are professional and sturdy, accessible for descendants to browse whenever they wish.

Another way to do this is to scan and position the photos in a document, type captions and context, and have a local copy shop make high-quality photocopies that you can have bound or slip the copies into sleeves within a three-ring binder. No matter who actually inherits the original wedding album, everyone will have a copy and be aware of the background!

## Category 2: Keep in extended family

Consult with relatives about items like the following, which might be classified in category 2:

*Duplicate photos and memorabilia.* If you have two photos of your parents cutting the wedding cake, or two photos of you and your sister in Halloween costumes, give one to your sibling or another member of your immediate family after digitizing it. Ditto for any family memorabilia that you have in duplicate.

*Photos or memorabilia of people not in your direct line.* Have photos of aunts, uncles, first cousins, or more distant relatives? If your family agrees, offer the originals to the people pictured (or to descendants of people pictured). This will build goodwill and downsize your collection, a plus for the next generation. A cousin was kind enough to give me the program from my mother's high school graduation. Good for her downsizing effort, and great for me and my genealogy collection! But do photograph or digitize items before you give them away.

*Duplicates or copies of family histories, family documents, etc.* If you have more than one of anything, consider giving the extras away to the people (or their descendants) mentioned in the documents. Even if you have to track somebody down to make the offer— especially if you have to track somebody down! Also consider donating copies of family histories to historical societies, genealogy libraries, and other repositories that welcome such publications. Match your donation to the institution, as explained in Chapter 7.

*Books, Bibles, other items with family names inscribed* or connected to the family's history. If you don't have room for the items, or you have more than one, ask family to help identify new caretakers. I gave away two religious books from my family's distant past, one to a niece and one to a cousin who appreciated the significance. In some cases, you may wish to donate such items to local historical or genealogical societies, local libraries, or other appropriate new homes.

## Managing family-first giveaways

For categories 1 and 2, identify a specific person (sibling, nephew, cousin, grandchild, etc.) for each item you want to give away. Contact that person, explain what you have, and explain why you believe it connects with that person's part of the family (if it's not obvious). If you're emailing, include a photo of the item.

In my experience, the first-choice person is often happy to accept what you want to give away. If not, approach another relative. Your collection will get smaller, and an item that belongs to someone else will be reunited with that family to be handed down to their descendants.

Giveaways strengthen your connections with others in your family. They're a great way to start or continue conversations about people from the past. You might even hear a new story as you reach out to cousins or family friends to offer duplicate or unneeded items. Someone you contact may actually tell a story to solve some mystery about your genealogy.

At the very least, giving items away means your relatives or family friends will have a tangible reminder of these ancestors. Your kindness in giving them a photo or artifact could help them start a genealogy conversation with *their* immediate families!

Here's an example: My mother saved a 1925 wedding photo of her aunt, dressed in a gown and floor-length veil. I scanned the photo in high resolution for my collection.

Next, I emailed it to my cousin, asking whether he would like this original portrait from his mother's wedding day. He said yes, I handed it to him a few weeks later, and he had good-quality copies made for his brother, sister, and children.

Seeing his mother's wedding photo prompted my cousin to talk about the fashionista aunt who designed and sewed dresses for our family's bridal parties during the 1930s and 1940s. My cousins gained a treasured photo, and I heard a new family story.

Do your recipients a special favor and put the photo or item into a protective sleeve or box. This will demonstrate the importance you place on the item, and encourage the recipient to treat it carefully.

For more ideas, listen to Amy Johnson Crow's podcast episode about downsizing (or read the succinct summary) at http://www.amyjohnsoncrow.com/downsizing-and-family-history/.

## Category 3: FAN club or family?

Category 3 is for items that can leave your family's hands. My collection originally included photos of children who were part of my family's FAN (friends, associates, neighbors) club. Notations served as clues, but I also checked with relatives before concluding that these were children of my parents' old friends or long-time neighbors.

With a little research, I located and contacted descendants of those in the photos. Not only did I downsize my collection, I also gave the photos to good new homes and helped those families fill in a bit of background from the past.

FAN club members sometimes turn out to be distant relations. The giveaway process forced me to research certain branches of my tree in more detail. It also gave me a concrete reason to get in touch and exchange information with these folks. In most cases, they knew a few tidbits that I could add to my captions.

Before you give away FAN club photos, do your homework, and investigate possible family connections. *Then* scan and give away these photos as part of your outreach effort. More about Category 3 items in Chapter 7.

## No cousin left behind

I strongly recommend coordinating with family members to save some photos or other items from cousins and other ancestors who had no descendants. It's possible that a few relatives could agree to accept some or all of the collection of these ancestors, so you don't have to store it all.

That's how I ended up with the wedding portrait and childhood photos of my second cousin Iris. She had no direct heirs; her collection went, by default, to her first cousin. That cousin asked me to take a few key items because of my interest in our family's genealogy. She also shared a few photos with another cousin who remembered Iris fondly.

Now a selection of Iris's photos will live on with my heirs, labeled and captioned so future generations understand who she was and how she was connected with my maternal grandmother's family. I want them to at least know Iris's name and her smile, even if they never knew her in person. No cousin left behind, no cousin forgotten in the future.

In Chapter 10, I'll explain what I did with items from my Aunt Dorothy's military service during World War II. She had no direct descendants. I wanted her to be remembered beyond the family, and my donation of her military items accomplished that purpose.

## To sum up:

√　Include family members in your decisions.

√　Sort items into three categories: *(1) keep* (in your collection or immediate family), *(2) keep* (in the extended family, not in your possession), *(3) find a good home elsewhere* (not in your family).

√　Make copies of one-of-a-kind items for multiple heirs.

√　Giveaways strengthen FAN and family connections and keep family history alive.

√　Find out whether FAN club members are actually family.

√　Coordinate with relatives to share photos and items from cousins and others with no direct descendants.

# CHAPTER 7
## FIND OUTSIDE HOMES FOR ARTIFACTS

In Chapter 6, you sorted your artifacts into categories and allocated family and FAN club ownership of items in categories 1 and 2. Now it's time to look at items in category 3, items that will *not* remain in your family's possession. Take time curating this category, because once items leave your family's hands, they will be gone forever.

## Category 3: Non-family homes for artifacts

Items in this category might be artifacts like old newspapers (saved from some historic event), school yearbooks, theater programs, military memorabilia, and so on. Think about the family significance, the historical significance, and the monetary value of each item. If these artifacts aren't directly related to your family history, you might want to find them a non-family home.

Consult with family when planning a future for these objects. Someone may want an item; someone may know a repository or an individual interested in an item; someone may have a strong opinion on the merits of selling versus donating, or even know a collector who would like to buy an item.

If you suspect an item is particularly valuable, you might want to ask a local auction house or antiques dealer for advice. Or you can get it appraised before you take the next step. Browse online for similar objects to get some sense of how unique and valuable your

43

item could be so you and your family can make an informed decision. (I'm not qualified to discuss items of value and whether they should be given away or sold.)

## Objects with minimal financial value

For artifacts with minimal monetary value, not essential to your family's past, think creatively about a new home. Would a historical society, college, museum, library, or an archive want such an item? These kinds of institutions are my personal preference for items not needed by the family. I really want my ancestors' possessions preserved for the long term, archived for study, or put on display.

For instance, my late father-in-law accumulated hundreds of theater programs from Broadway shows spanning six decades. No one in the family wanted them. A cousin located a state university that was pleased to accept these programs for its drama library. I've since used online searches to locate other libraries that collect programs, and donated dozens more, with a brief bio and photo of my dad-in-law.

Another example: my husband inherited a war bond wallet embossed with General Douglas MacArthur's likeness. It had little financial or sentimental value, but it was of some small historical significance.

I approached two World War II museums, but none would accept it, in part because a war bond wallet is not unusual or exceptional.

After a bit more research, I found a good home for the wallet, as you'll see in a moment.

## Preparing to donate to an institution

If you and your family decide to try and donate an object to an institution, you'll need to:

*Photograph* the item from several angles (for the repository and for your records).

*Evaluate* the item's condition so you can describe it in detail.

*Measure* the item's size, shape, and weight.

*Document* the provenance. How long has the object been in the family? When and how was it originally acquired?

*Summarize* what the item is about with a "30-second pitch" (written or oral) that you can use when contacting an institution.

Every institution will ask these questions, so be prepared before you email, call, or write a letter. Remember, you must ask permission to donate. And you (or someone in your family) must be the legal owner so you can transfer ownership to a repository.

## Match the item to the institution

Don't make my rookie mistake and email the Smithsonian Institution in Washington, D.C. about donating an item related to U.S. history. It gets flooded with inquiries. After hearing nothing for months, I found out curators reply only if they're interested. The objects I wanted to donate were not significant enough to be considered.

To identify possible institutions, think about your item's background. The war bond wallet was from World War II, which led me to investigate U.S. military museums. The wallet didn't belong to someone serving in the war, however, which is why two WWII museums weren't interested. But the face of General MacArthur gave me another idea (more later).

Does your item relate to a particular country, state, county, or town, or even a particular building? Does it have meaning for historical or religious reasons? What kinds of researchers or historians might want access to it? Does the local library have a genealogy collection or does the local history society welcome such items?

Try an online search. Most repositories like museums and historical societies have an online page explaining how to make contact regarding possible donations of items. They often describe exactly what types of items they are interested in, and any requirements for donating an item.

For instance, the Western Reserve Historical Society in Cleveland, Ohio describes the types of items it would like to receive, how its donation process works, and the names of curators (www.wrhs.org/research/donating-materials/). Similarly, the New England Historic Genealogical Society website (www.americanancestors.org/give/donate-materials) describes the kinds of materials it accepts as donations, along with contact info for its archivist. Another example: the National Museums Scotland website explains the donation process and provides a donation form helping curators to assess the item (see www.nms.ac.uk/support-us/donate-an-object/).

## Contacting an institution

Once you identify a possible institution and understand its requirements, get in touch by phone or email. In your initial contact, explain what the item is, its size and condition, and the provenance and significance (your 30-second pitch). Repositories welcome inquiries and usually follow up. The answer is not always "yes," but most will respond.

When you contact an institution, be ready to answer additional questions, such as whether the item has ever been changed or restored. Before a repository formally accepts a donation, it needs internal approvals, which can take days or weeks. Then the institution will ask you how you plan to transport the item, either by personally delivering it or sending it another way. This is your responsibility.

The repository will send you paperwork documenting your transfer of ownership. Read about the U.S. legal form "deed of gift" (or "contract of gift") at the Society of American Archivists (https://tinyurl.com/2reecxzd). You'll be signing a document similar to this when you donate.

Be sure to keep digital images of items you've given away. In the future, a descendant might want to know what the family donated and where it is. You can position a digital photo of the item on a page and type a few lines about the provenance, print it or electronically file it with your records. Keeping a written record takes up much less space than the item itself. This is a story your genealogical heirs might want to know.

By the way, many repositories appreciate a brief bio of the ancestor whose artifact you're donating. I also send an ancestor photo along with a bio when donating an item. I encourage my family to think of our ancestor(s) being represented in the collections of these repositories, their names and faces linked to these artifacts.

## Successful donations

Here are two examples of how I donated items to repositories.

***WWII war bond wallet showing General MacArthur.*** After being rejected by two WWII museums, I did another online search and found the website of the MacArthur Memorial Museum in Virginia. Following the museum's instructions for potential donations, I emailed photos of the item to the curator, explaining the provenance (my father-in-law received the wallet from a Cleveland business in the early 1940s). Museum officials quickly agreed to accept the wallet. Within two weeks, hubby had signed the deed of gift and we express-shipped the wallet to its new home. We plan to visit the museum some time when we are in Norfolk, Virginia.

***Ledger books and letters from the late 1800s.*** These weren't actually family items, I discovered through research (but I have a good idea of how my father came into possession). I traced the names using the U.S. Census and city directories. When I learned that the families were from Ossining, New York, I contacted the Ossining Historical Society Museum. Its directors recognized the surnames as prominent families from the past, and they accepted the ledgers for their collection.

## Tax implications? Ask an expert!

Sorry—I'm definitely *not* an expert, and can offer no guidance on this issue, or the legalities of giving items to repositories. Please check with the institution and your tax advisor about whether your donations have tax implications, and how to document such transfers accordingly.

As noted above, photograph anything you donate. Also keep all your correspondence (print out emails, for example) so you'll have a paper trail if you need one.

## To sum up:

√ Consult with family members about whether to sell, give away, or donate items.

√ Think creatively about placing objects (those with minimal financial value) with appropriate repositories.

√ If you plan to donate, photograph and measure the item and then document its provenance.

√ Match the item to the institution and understand how the institution prefers to be approached.

√ Use your 30-second pitch when asking permission to donate.

√ Be prepared to legally transfer ownership to the institution.

√ Let family members know where items have been placed.

√ Get expert advice about tax and legal implications.

# CHAPTER 8
## WHO WANTS YOUR
## GENEALOGY COLLECTION?

You really don't want your cherished collection of family photos and old documents to wind up in a flea market, an online auction, or (gasp!) a dumpster. Nor should tomorrow's family historians have to start from scratch when you already have a collection of genealogical materials to share with them.

This chapter, which begins Step 3 in the PASS process, will put you on the path to designating heirs for your family history. The earlier you plan ahead and document your wishes, the better.

If you have no obvious heirs for your collection, there are still steps you can take now to find safe homes for photos, research, heirlooms, and other items. See Chapter 10 for more on this topic.

### Identify future custodians

Start with your immediate family: If you have adult children (or nieces or nephews or grandchildren), would they be good future caretakers for your family history materials? If you're searching for custodians outside your immediate family, you may want to think about cousins (one or more) who've shown interest at some point.

Also consider identifying a separate heir for your mother's and father's side of the family if you want documents, photos, or other items passed down separately.

Ask yourself: **(1)** Who in the next generation is interested (even mildly) in family history? **(2)** Who in the next generation would be a careful custodian? **(3)** Who in the next generation might continue the research at some point in the future?

Fortunately, I have a volunteer from both sides of the family to take custody of all the archived records, files, photos, albums, heirlooms, family tree data, and DNA results.

These future custodians have been briefed on who's who in the family, and they've heard the stories. They've seen where the archival boxes and file cabinets are located; they have copies of pedigree charts and access to my online trees and DNA results (with website info and passwords). They're willing to take over when the time comes. It's possible that these heirs will continue the research when they have more time in the coming years.

I'm also leaving each of these heirs a little money to help them preserve the materials for the first couple of years. Let me suggest you consider doing the same as part of your genealogical "will" (more about that in Chapter 9). The idea is to make it as appealing as possible for heirs to say "yes" to accepting the collection.

## Ask permission to bequeath

It's very important to ask permission to bequeath your collection—you don't want your materials in limbo if someone you've designated is unwilling or unable to accept the responsibility.

Have a conversation with the potential custodians you've identified, stressing that your family's history and the materials you've collected are important. As part of the family's past, they should also be part of the family's future.

Explain that the genealogy collection you've spent years assembling is organized (or soon will be, right?). Reassure potential heirs that everything will be clearly labeled by family, to avoid any confusion. Remind them of safe storage practices.

Also let potential heirs know whether you think others in the family might want to be involved, either as researchers or as shared custodians. Maybe they'll chat with relatives and team up. Just getting a conversation going within the family is a good thing, and can spark interest in learning more.

## Smooth the way for heirs

Anticipate questions your identified heirs may ask, and be ready with answers. Maybe space is an issue, or money, or family feuds over certain objects. Whatever the obstacle, try to smooth the way *now* so your collection will go to the best possible custodian(s) when the time comes.

Don't allow unfamiliar technology to be a barrier for your future custodians. Although many in the next generation are tech-savvy, you don't want your heirs to worry about learning *your* technology. You may love the software or genealogy websites you use, but your heirs might be put off by a steep learning curve. They have lives of their own, and might not want to invest as much time as we have in researching and documenting family history. Or, conversely, they may prefer online trees rather than a lot of paper.

If technology is a potential stumbling block, look at alternatives—printing family trees and pedigrees, for instance, or leaving money to perpetuate a subscription until the heirs can get up to speed or transfer family tree details elsewhere.

The point is to make it as easy as possible for identified heirs to take possession of your collection after you join your ancestors, and to preserve your collection for future generations.

No obvious heirs? See Chapter 10 for ideas that can help keep your collection from going into the recycle bin.

## What and where?

Let the heirs know which of the following they should expect to receive from your collection (when they inherit in the far future):

- *Photographs and home movies* (separated by family and captioned or annotated, if possible; include "mystery" and "unknown" photos, slides, negatives, etc., preferably with tentative captions indicating your best guess of who and where).
- *Family histories* (printed and/or digital).
- *Diaries, letters, and notebooks* from ancestors and relatives.
- *Online family trees and DNA results* (online addresses and passwords too).
- *Genealogy correspondence* with relatives, societies, etc.

- *Bibles, heirlooms, and other tangible items* from the family's past (and indicate if you're donating any items, just in case).
- *Notes about ancestors* and other items within the collection.
- *Computer files, external hard drives, USB drives,* other tech media containing genealogical data.
- *Cloud backups* of your genealogy (passwords).
- *Audio and video recordings* of interviews with relatives or family friends (on media or digitized).
- *Listings of burial places for ancestors* (online or in print).
- *Anything else that should remain* with the genealogy collection, such as heirlooms or artifacts.
- *Highlights of family history* (Mayflower ancestors, early immigrants, ancestral home towns, other key info not to be lost).

Also remember that your collection needs to look organized and important enough to save for the future. If you bequeath a jumble, heirs may not perceive the vital nuggets of family history you're leaving to them for safekeeping. Get the collection organized, and they will be more encouraged to preserve the family's past.

## Share ancestors' burial places

Future generations should be aware of where ancestors are buried. You can share this information by including funeral cards and other printed materials in a special folder. Or you can prepare a list and slide it into a folder or a digital file.

Knowing that my family prefers electronic sharing, I created a free virtual cemetery on FindaGrave.com (www.findagrave.com) where I grouped memorial pages for ancestors on each side of the family. I can email a link to each virtual cemetery and download the listing of memorials for my own files. This way, the location of ancestral burial places will be remembered by those in the future.

## Share your cousin connections

Don't forget to share a list of living cousins with your collection. Each of my parents (and grandparents) had many cousins—some I never met or even heard of before starting my genealogy research.

In some cases, my research led me to descendants of older cousins who were unaware of our relationship until I got in touch.

To document my cousin connections, I created a table with three columns. In the first, I listed living cousins by surname, indicating relationship with the name. In the second column, I entered contact info. The third column was for notes, such as when I saw or talked with the cousin most recently. I dated the list and I change the date when I add new information (often noting changes by hand until I can update digitally). The list is sortable by surname, a plus (see sample).

I want my relatives and heirs to know about all of our cousins, hoping they'll stay in touch in the future. This listing comes in handy when I find new cousins and want to see who else shares that surname or maiden name. However, be sensitive to the privacy concerns of your cousins. If you want to put cousins in contact now, first ask each person's permission before disclosing any details.

## Sample cousin connection listing

| NAME | CONTACT INFO | NOTES |
|---|---|---|
| **Surname, Given**<br><br>(maiden name: ___ )<br>(relationship: ______ ) | 892 Street Name<br>City, State, Country,<br>Postal Code<br>Phone<br>Email | Daughter of Sally Sample. Her mother was at Marian's wedding in 19xx. Marian last visited with her in 2019. |

## To sum up:

√   Identify potential heirs for your genealogy collection.

√   Ask permission to bequeath, explaining the importance of family history.

√   Anticipate and try to overcome obstacles that might cause an heir not to accept your collection.

√   Tell heirs what they should expect to receive.

√   Plan to leave heirs an organized collection that looks

important enough to preserve for the future.
√ Document genealogical highlights and ancestor burial places.
√ Prepare a list of living cousin connections so these relationships are known to the next generation.

# CHAPTER 9
## WRITE YOUR GENEALOGICAL "WILL"

To be sure your designated heirs receive your collection, you need to explain, in writing, what you plan for the future of your family history. This is a vital part of Step 3 in the PASS process.

However, if you have no clear heirs for your family history, please read Chapter 10 for ideas and steps you should take soon, before you join your ancestors.

**PLEASE NOTE:** The sample "will" included in this chapter is only a *sample* format, for general information only. Nothing in this book should be construed as legal advice or legal opinion. Please consult with an expert about what is best for your unique situation.

### Four reasons to write a genealogical "will"

Here are the top four reasons to document your plan for the genealogical materials you've worked so hard to acquire:

**1.** To alert your family and the legal executor of your estate about specific instructions regarding what happens to your genealogical collection.

**2.** To remind family and future custodians of the extent of your collection and the importance of keeping it safe for the future.

**3.** To request a waiting period, allowing time to identify suitable custodians if your designated heirs can't or won't accept the responsibility.

**4.** To suggest alternative people and institutions to be contacted about accepting part or all of your genealogical collection, if your designated custodians don't accept your collection intact.

Do your homework and be prepared well in advance.

## What to include in a genealogical "will"

Exactly what you say in your written instructions depends on the arrangements you've made with your designated heirs and your family. For example, the sample "will" shown in this book has spaces to list heirs to be contacted and institutions that might be interested if your designated heirs can't or won't take possession.

You may want to include more detail in your instructions. Ideally, include inventory sheets or possibly photos of your artifacts and collection with your written document. You may even mention DNA results and family trees on genealogy websites. The goal is to be sure heirs know exactly what they should have and which heirs get which part of the collection.

The sample "will" in this chapter emphasizes the importance of holding onto the collection for two years, because of the time, effort, and expense involved in researching the family tree. It also notes that the collection should be preserved to allow for further research and study. Even if family members aren't interested, institutions may find value in the materials you've collected. These are good points to mention in your written instructions and in discussions with your family.

If you like, indicate in your written instructions that you want your heirs to receive a small amount of money for the first year or two. Your heirs might appreciate receiving money to pay for access to a fee-based genealogy website, or to buy new genealogy software, or to buy additional archival boxes or other storage materials.

Compared with the value of the collection (to you and to your family's future), leaving some money to care for your materials is a worthy investment! Be sure to indicate, in writing, how much money each heir is to receive and for how long (or a lump sum when they inherit family history materials).

## SAMPLE Genealogical "will" for preserving family history

To my spouse, children and/or heirs, guardian, administrator or executor:

Upon my death, it is requested that you DO NOT dispose of any or all of my genealogical records, both those prepared personally, and those prepared by others, which may be in my possession. This includes but is not limited to books, paper and/or computer files, notebooks, correspondence, audio/visual items, photographs, and documents, for a period of two years.

During this two-year period, please attempt to identify one or more persons who would be willing to take custody of said materials and the responsibility of maintaining and continuing the family histories.

Parties to contact regarding the assumption of the custody of these items include but are not limited to:

**NAME**               **ADDRESS**               **PHONE/EMAIL**

_______________________________________________________________

In the event that you find no one to accept these materials, please contact the institutions listed below, in order, and determine if they will accept part or all of my genealogical materials.

**INSTITUTION**     **ADDRESS/CONTACT**     **PHONE/EMAIL**

_______________________________________________________________

Please remember that my family history studies consumed a great deal of time, travel, and money. Therefore, it is my strong desire that the product of these efforts be preserved and allowed to continue in a manner that will make them available to others in the future.

Signature                              Witness

______________________                 ______________________

(name)________________                 (name) ________________

Date _________________                 Date __________________

NOTE: This sample genealogical "will" is adapted and reprinted with the kind permission of the *Devon Family History Society*.

To see samples of genealogical "wills," do an online search. Here are two links as a starting point. Remember—these are only **samples**, and may not work for you, as written. You should consult a legal advisor about the best approach for your family.

www.devonfhs.org.uk/my-genealogical-will.pdf *(This is a document posted on the Devon Family History Society website)*

dillmanfamilyassociation.org/pdf/genwill.pdf *(This is a document posted on the Dillman Family Association website)*

## Think about your own situation

When writing your wishes, think about how the rest of your family will feel about your plans. Have that discussion with the various heirs before you sit down to write your "will" if you're concerned about conflict over who gets which materials. Also emphasize how important it is to keep family history alive for future generations.

Not everyone can have an original photo or document, if more than one heir covets something like your parents' wedding album. I suggested earlier that you make good copies of unique items like this. Then your heirs will have a copy without breaking up the original. You can also recreate family photo albums by scanning the pages or specific photos and printing photo books for multiple heirs.

Your genealogical "will" should mention who gets the original, together with other originals currently in your collection. Show your future custodians where your collection is located and give them inventory sheets or other paperwork to hold "just in case." Remind them you're bequeathing original photos, albums, and other materials in the proper storage containers (archival boxes, for example) for long-term preservation.

Be sure heirs know how to access your digital data (family trees, backups, DNA results, etc.). If any institutions are to receive one or more items from your collection, make your custodians aware of these arrangements, preferably in writing to avoid any misunderstandings. If you have already donated items to a repository, have copies of the deeds of gift with your genealogical will or within your collection, so future generations will know which institutions now have those artifacts.

As part of your plan, consider what happens to your "will." Are you going to leave written instructions with your legal will? Put a copy with your genealogical collection? Leave a copy with your attorney and with the designated heirs?

## Have a contingency plan

Sometimes life gets in the way of the most careful planning. Include a contingency plan with your "will" in the event your chosen custodians are unwilling or unable to accept your collection when the time comes.

The last thing you want is for your collection, built with care over the years, to wind up in the rubbish.

Some ideas to consider for a contingency plan:

*Find a secondary heir* who will step up if absolutely no one else does so. This might be a cousin or another relative. List this secondary heir's contact info in the "will," along with your preferred custodians. Also note what part of the collection the secondary heir(s) will accept.

*Suggest one or more institutions* that might be willing to accept part or all of your collection. Again, list these institutions (with the names of people to contact, ideally) in your "will." Do your homework before listing any institution!

*Mention that your collection* should not be stowed away in a damp basement, hot attic, or musty garage while decisions are being made. By the time a custodian takes possession, the materials you've worked so hard to protect might be damaged if not stored in appropriate conditions. If you think this could be a possibility, have a conversation with heirs now.

The ultimate goal of writing a genealogical "will" is to keep your collection of family-history research files, old photos, and other items safe for the future, in the family or in a repository.

## One piece at a time

If you have silverware, fine china, jewelry, or other sets of valuable or sentimental items like these, consider offering relatives one place setting, one teaspoon, or one bracelet. Or offer one of anything you've inherited. Family members might not have space for many items, but would likely want one item as a memento of an ancestor, for instance.

Be creative in sharing artifacts like these so some remain in the family for the future. Leave them in your genealogical "will" or give them away right now. They may be of more interest to recipients if you share a family story or photo of ancestor(s) who owned/used the item.

## To sum up:

√　Create a written plan for your genealogical collection so the materials survive into the future.

√　List heirs, list institutions, include inventories or other details about what's in the collection and where it's located.

√　Consider leaving heirs a little money to help care for the collection.

√　Think about your family's reaction to your plans.

√　Have a contingency plan (or more than one), just in case.

√　Consider offering relatives a teaspoon, a place setting of china, or a set of cufflinks, to keep a few items in the family.

# CHAPTER 10
## NO OBVIOUS HEIRS? TRY THESE IDEAS

Sometimes there are no obvious heirs for part or all of your genealogy collection. You still have some paths forward, as this chapter explains. It's up to you to investigate specific ideas before you make any final decisions about your collection. Keep your personal situation in mind as you read about actions you might take, now and in the near future, as part of Step 3 in the PASS process.

## Background on donating a collection

For important background, check this page on Family Search describing options for donating a personal genealogy collection: https://tinyurl.com/pfx9xwjj.

Here's more detail about what the Family History Library will accept for its collection: https://tinyurl.com/68a2uvf.

Also read this page from the Society of American Archivists, which explains how and why to donate an entire personal genealogy collection: https://tinyurl.com/j88bxkk3.

Another society that is willing to accept a personal genealogy collection, under some circumstances, is the UK-based Society of Genealogists. Check its website for information and contacts to learn more about its holdings and collecting interests: https://sog.org.uk.

As you can see, some institutions may be willing to accept all or much of your collection. Still, I strongly recommend thinking about giving relatives particularly significant family history items before you place the entire collection elsewhere, out of the family's hands.

## Ask a niece, nephew, or cousin

Are you in touch with nieces, nephews, first cousins, or more distant cousins (on either side of your family)? One or more than one of these relatives might be willing to accept a few key items from your genealogy collection.

In my experience, nephews/nieces/cousins are generally willing to hold onto a family portrait that includes their parents/ancestors. Maybe you have a group portrait from a family wedding or reunion. Even if the photo was taken fairly recently rather than decades in the past, ask whether your relative would kindly take possession of the original for the sake of future generations. If you have more than one interested relative, digitize so all can have the captioned photo and share stories with their heirs.

If a certain relative was especially close to your parents or to a grandparent, ask that person to safeguard some or all of your family history collection. Maybe your relative would agree to accept a few photos, documents, and other materials related to a favorite ancestor.

Another idea: contact a cousin or niece or nephew who has some engagement with family history. Explain that you want to avoid having your research and items lost to future generations. This relative may be persuaded to hold some or all of your collection, keeping it safe and finding other relatives to continue safeguarding the collection later.

## Offer one item

So many people seem to be trying to find heirs for fine china and silverware. It turns out the younger generation may not have interest in or space for fine china for 12 or a full set of silverware or goblets. Yet these items were precious to our ancestors, set out proudly on special occasions, and we want them safe for the future. I mentioned this briefly in the previous chapter, but let me recap here in case you have no obvious heirs.

Try asking relatives whether they would like to have a *single* teaspoon or teacup, a *single* place setting of china, or a *single* piece of jewelry from your family's past. Perhaps they will admire the design or enjoy the vintage look of these items. These days, "mix and match" is shabby chic in some circles. Or you can offer one of any set of items that you would like to keep in the family, along with the story of why it's special.

A few younger folks might appreciate a tangible reminder of a person or a family occasion they remember, such as a big holiday dinner. Everyone has space for a single teaspoon or one of any set. It's worth a try. And this approach may work for other items from your ancestors, such as collectibles or hand-made objects.

## Placing a collection in non-family hands

If you decide to give your family-history collection to an institution, think about how to describe its significance. What does your collection exemplify, in terms of genealogy and history? What story does it tell about a particular place or period, a group of people, a specific situation or experience? Did your ancestors keep scrapbooks, photo albums, or other items that help tell the story? Is your collection unique in some way?

What might researchers learn by looking at your collection? Does your collection include unusual personal items or hard-to-find original records that you've managed to acquire? Did your ancestors have a brush with history, fame, notoriety, or some landmark event? Were they representative of a larger movement or living through a momentous time in history such as the Great Depression or the U.S. Civil War?

Institutions are most interested in *original* items in your collection. Judy Lucey, Senior Archivist for the New England Historic Genealogical Society, explains: "Archives want to collect documents and materials that have historic value as well as research value for their users, so original documents such as family and bible records, documents created during one's lifetime (such as school records, letters, diaries, business records, estate papers, land records, photographs), and genealogical records all have historic and research value." For more about donating items to the NEHGS, see www.americanancestors.org/give/donate-materials.

Before you approach any institution, write a few sentences describing your collection, indicating its significance in a "30-second pitch." Also summarize the main surnames, places, years covered, types of materials, and anything else a repository should know about the collection. When an institution asks about your collection, you'll have a concise and compelling explanation.

Remember, non-family eyes will be looking at your collection. Preparing a family tree or pedigree chart will help any institution better understand the relationships among ancestors whose files you are donating. Ideally, organize your collection a bit before you begin the donation process and use your 30-second pitch as an overview.

## Investigating potential institutions

Based on the scope and significance of your collection, begin an online search for appropriate institutions that might consider accepting your family's history. Look at libraries, museums, archives, genealogical societies, historical societies, or other repositories in areas where your ancestors lived or worked or that in some way relate to your ancestors' backgrounds.

Out-of-area institutions may have a research interest in aspects of your collection, so cast a wide net at first. Next, click around the website of each repository to find out about its collection, its donation policies, and the best person to contact with an inquiry.

As an example, the website of the Newberry Library in Chicago (www.newberry.org/) reflects its far-reaching collection interests beyond genealogies from Illinois and the United States. Its holdings include Canadian and British Isles resources, travel materials, and

Latin American history materials, among other categories.

The Society of Genealogists (https://sog.org.uk/) seeks unique, original documents and research material (not downloaded records or document copies). This society prefers a brief description (a 30-second pitch) of your collection as part of the process. Browse its website to understand its collecting focus before getting in touch.

Once you have possibilities in mind, consider which would be the best fit for your collection. Then begin making contact. If one institution is not interested, ask for suggestions about another institution that might be appropriate. I encourage you to explore a number of possibilities until you find a repository that will accept some or all of your collection. Be sure you understand the institution's requirements before signing the legal documents to donate your collection.

## Remember those without descendants

Before you place your entire collection, you may want to separate specific photos, documents, or artifacts connected with an ancestor who had no descendants. It's possible that other relatives would agree to hold a few items if they remember that ancestor or admire that ancestor's accomplishments. Just ask, and see what happens.

If you don't wish to have a relative hold this ancestor's materials, or can't find a relative to hold them, consider finding a safe new home in an institution, possibly apart from the rest of the collection.

Let me share what I did with my aunt Dorothy's military memorabilia. She joined the U.S. Army Women's Army Corps during World War II. Later, she was the historian of her unit. Not only did I have the printed history she wrote, I had her Bronze Star citation, news clippings about her service, and other documents.

Since Dorothy had no descendants, and the materials in my collection were specialized, I wanted to keep her memory alive by donating to a suitable repository. First, I listed what I wanted to donate. Then, I thought about her role as a U.S. Army WAC, a World War II veteran, and a female military veteran.

Doing an online search of these categories, I quickly discovered the U.S. Army Women's Museum located in Fort Lee, Virginia (https://awm.lee.army.mil/). The website states: "We are actively collecting the stories of female soldiers (Active Duty,

National Guard, and Reserve) and DA civilians." The museum also conducts oral histories and collects biographical info about women in the Army. After an email exchange with a curator, my sister and I decided this was the place to donate our aunt's military materials.

One of the best things about this donation is that the museum provided a detailed biographical questionnaire, with plenty of space for me to share information about my aunt's life before, during, and after her wartime service. I also shared some genealogical background and two photos of my aunt in uniform. My family feels good about placing this aunt's military materials in a safe new home where her service will be remembered and honored, and available to future researchers.

If you have ancestors without direct descendants, and especially if there are specialized materials associated with these ancestors, please do consider the question of donating these materials separately from the entire collection. You don't have to donate separately—it's up to you as you write your plan for the future of your collection. It's just an option for you to keep in mind.

## To sum up:

√   Do your homework on donating a personal genealogy collection before making any decisions.
√   Try relatives first before approaching any institution.
√   Offer a single place setting or single teaspoon to relatives as a way to keep some keepsakes in the family.
√   If planning to donate your collection, describe its scope and significance, with emphasis on original items.
√   Investigate potential institutions and understand their collection interests and legal requirements.
√   Consider whether to separately donate materials from ancestors without direct descendants to a suitable repository.

# CHAPTER 11
## KEEP FAMILY HISTORY ALIVE

In Step 4 of the PASS process, you'll be sharing what you've learned about family history with members of the next generation and with the wider world, to keep the names, stories, and memories alive.

This chapter is just a starting point for breathing life into the names and dates on your family tree. Use your imagination and adapt ideas to your family's particular interests. Also consider how to share your genealogy online, with privacy in mind, as another way to keep family history alive for the future.

**Know your family audience**

What are your relatives interested in? When my husband talked about his McClure ancestor being a civic leader and possibly a distant relation of a McClure who was supposedly a villain, our grandchildren sighed. They wished the *outlaw* had been their ancestor, not the upstanding citizen!

Most of us don't have a bandit or pirate in our family tree, but surely there's something to grab the attention of relatives. For example:

- Was your ancestor the first in the family or the town to do something (such as found a church or buy the first TV)? Or the last to do something (the last carpenter in a line of carpenters)?
- Was your ancestor an inventor, an entrepreneur, a bandmaster,

or in an unusual occupation?

- Did your ancestor live on a farm, in a tenement, or someplace different from where the family lives now?
- Was your ancestor involved in something historic, such as serving in a war or working as a "Rosie the Riveter"?
- Did your ancestor write, paint, sew, sing, play music, perform, or have another talent that runs in the family?
- Was your ancestor unusually educated for the time? Could your ancestor even read or write?
- Which ancestors never left the home country? Which ancestors moved from country to country, and why?

## Use photos to intrigue

Get out that box of photos and see what you can do to intrigue the next generation. For example, you can show family portraits from the past, side-by-side with family portraits of today . . . and ask which of the younger generation looks the most like Grandpa and Grandma (or Great-grandma, etc.).

Point out unusual elements in an old family portrait, such as a pocket watch still in the family or a silly costume worn by a solemn ancestor. Ask about the old fashions or bushy beards. Display photos of old birthday parties. Hey, Nana was young once, and she celebrated birthdays, too.

Show youngsters a picture of the ship ancestors boarded to leave the old country or an old steam engine from an ancestral era. Ask what they think ancestors ate, wore, or felt like during the journey. Did ancestors know what awaited them at their destination? Did they speak the language or have relatives or friends to take them in? Were your ancestors expecting to go home again? Did anyone from the home country send photos or gifts to their immigrant relatives?

## Take a field trip

The next generation might be interested in learning more about their journey-taker ancestors—and the hardships or heartbreaks along the way. Can you take them on a field trip?

My immigrant ancestors arrived at Castle Garden and Ellis Island in New York City, more than a century in the past. Not too long ago, my sister and I, along with cousins, took a field trip to Ellis Island (www.statueofliberty.org/ellis-island/). We had several immigrant ancestors listed on Ellis Island's impressive "Wall of Honor" (www.statueofliberty.org/support/wall-of-honor/).

It was inspiring to look at names on the wall, and hear people of all ages talking about their immigrant roots. We'll take the younger generation along on a future trip. Meanwhile, they've seen photos of our visit (more than once).

It's easy to take the next generation along on a virtual field trip, via Google, for example. Here's a family photo from 1911, showing my late father-in-law and his brother in front of a home that their father built in Cleveland, Ohio.

The house is still standing and looks much the same, I found by doing a Google search for the exact address. Descendants were impressed that the house was sturdy enough to remain intact for generations, and of handsome design as well.

## Tell the stories

Every family has stories. Sometimes the stories are forgotten through the generations, as with my husband's Mayflower ancestry. Then a contemporary cousin rediscovered that lineage and it ignited some interest in the family's distant past.

You can tell the stories in different ways to different audiences: In conversations (at a meal or a family occasion), through a family-history blog, in letters and greeting cards, in a video call, whenever you have the opportunity.

I send my grandchildren a Thanksgiving card each year, noting: "You had five Mayflower ancestors: Degory Priest, Mary Norris

Allerton, Isaac Allerton, Mary Allerton, and Francis Cooke." Year after year, this is a reminder of a key part of the family's history that shouldn't be lost.

Play up the drama of your family's stories to make family history more memorable. Here's the short version of a story from my family tree. "My Grandma Minnie refused an arranged marriage favored by her parents. She threw the suitor's engagement ring out the window (but her brothers ran downstairs to pick it up)." What happened to the ring? No one alive today knows. Just asking the question adds to the drama of the story.

What drama can you emphasize in your stories? Think of ancestors' goals, dreams, failures, achievements, health, happiness, luck, love, and other elements that reveal personality and humanity. Perhaps the journey from the old country to the new country was dramatic in some way, or the fate of relatives left behind was dramatic. Unusual personality quirks can add drama, as can pithy quotes about or by the ancestor. See how you can bring ancestors to life with stories featuring these kinds of details.

## Bite-sized family history

Whether you want to share family history with relatives or share with the wider world online, I encourage you to do this with bite-sized projects that can be finished in a short time. The key is to narrow your focus to one ancestor or a couple, a set of siblings, a particular family or surname, one special occasion, one family photo or heirloom, or a special place from family history.

Not only can you print or distribute a bite-sized project digitally, you can repurpose content in other ways. Remember to maintain the privacy of living people, and respect copyright law pertaining to photos not taken by your family for personal use. Also understand the terms of service for online sites, how they can use your content.

Write a couple of sentences or paragraphs, based on your research, and think of how to add visual interest. For my father-in-law's bite-sized bio, I included a quote from an interview conducted decades ago. It reflected his determination to go to college and illuminated his relationship with his father, who was against the college idea. The photo was from my dad-in-law's passport, and the signature added a nice touch. Over time, I've been sharing this brief bio on various genealogy sites, without naming those still living.

On my side of the tree, I wrote two brief paragraphs about my father's life, emphasizing his goal of becoming a travel agent and how his career was interrupted by his Army service in World War II. I included his parents' names and dates, my Mom's name and dates, and other details, plus a photo of Dad in uniform.

After sharing with relatives, I posted my Dad's bio and photo on Fold3.com (www.fold3.com) to honor his military service. Also, I posted the bio on his memorial page at FindaGrave.com (www.findagrave.com), with the terms of service in mind.

## Family history coloring book

After reading Lisa A. Alzo's ideas for an ancestor coloring book (see article at https://bit.ly/3leAdpe), I created one as a fun bite-sized project for all ages. For this project, scan photos of a particular person, a couple, or one line of your tree, make them black-and-white, and use the "sketch" or "pencil sketch" function in your photo software to deemphasize dark areas and lighten light areas.

Low-tech option: put a photo on a copier and adjust the contrast until the dark areas are less dense and light areas are lighter.

Then, place one or two photos on a single page, list name(s), and indicate relationship to the recipient ("Isaac Burk, your great-grandfather"). Provide a printed copy and a digital copy so adults can reprint for more coloring fun in the future. To try making your own, another resource is Lisa Louise Cooke's how-to post (https://tinyurl.com/ss6rcxs).

## Family history booklets

After collecting a lot of research about my family's past, I created a 10-page booklet about my maternal grandparents, including photos and maps to show where they lived and moved during their lives. I also included an abbreviated tree showing grandma and grandpa's parents and grandparents, and wrote the story of their arrival in America from Hungary, their courtship, and their married life in the Bronx, New York.

To add to the written bio, I scanned vital documents (their marriage license and his naturalization certificate, for example). But my main point was to help the next generation understand these ancestors as human beings, what they hoped to achieve by making a new start in New York City, who they left behind, how they made a living, and how they raised a family.

Putting my grandparents into a social and historical context was important. I mentioned a bit about the world my grandparents were born into: Electricity was not in widespread use; horses were a common method of transportation; the United States had only 38 states. Younger relatives were taken aback by the idea of living without electricity, let alone without email or texting!

You don't have to spend a lot to print your family history. I digitally arranged the text, photos, and maps in a document. The local copy shop printed it, in color, on good paper. Then I put the pages into clear protective sleeves and sent them to relatives, to store in a binder along with other biographies I occasionally send. Another idea is to share electronically rather than in print.

## Resources for writing

For resources to help you write about ancestors and family history, check out these links:
- The Genealogy Center at the Allen County Public Library (how and why to record your family's story, at https://youtu.be/bocz3gw-Udk)
- Family Search (how to create a family history at

https://tinyurl.com/rmrrvthj).
- The New York Public Library (why write family history at https://tinyurl.com/4wr2y56p).
- The U.S. Library of Congress (writing a family history and submitting to the Library of Congress, at https://tinyurl.com/c9h5ps6f).
- Family Tree UK magazine (first steps to writing family history, at https://tinyurl.com/nmwkuxjs).
- Devon Lee from Family History Fanatics (top tips for writing family history and keeping it simple, at www.youtube.com/watch?v=cvoshRhzVcU).

## Video or audio family history

Depending on your audience, you may want to create a video-based project focusing on one ancestor or a couple, one surname or one line in your family tree, or a special heirloom/photo/occasion/place from family history. Younger relatives in particular may prefer video rather than a page or a booklet filled with text.

Video gives you a great opportunity to engage your audience and tell your family's story in a dynamic way, props and all, alone or with a relative. Do an online search for video apps or genealogy sites that offer video for family history— tech changes so often that I can't recommend a specific one here. Or consider a video call or videoconference. You can record yourself or a relative or both of you, discussing a focus occasion or specific ancestor.

Prepare by planning content in advance, knowing the story you want to tell, and having props (heirlooms or photos, for instance) at hand. You might develop a slide show that you record as you narrate each slide. Or you ask a relative to talk about a specific genealogical highlight during a video conference as you share your screen with old photos or a slide show of family history.

Another alternative to written family history is an oral history, or recording an interview with a relative or family friend. This can be done in person or remotely. Before you begin, have a list of mainly open-ended questions or prompts for the interviewee. You want to hear what this relative has to say, so allow time for each answer.

If your interviewee doesn't answer a question immediately, wait a minute or two. Especially if you're asking questions about the distant past, it takes extra time to retrieve old memories. Be patient!

After an audio interview, I recommend transcribing it so you have a paper-based record. Even if audio tech changes, you'll always have the transcription to share with future generations.

For more ideas about audio and video family history, see:

- The Genealogy Center at the Allen County Public Library (links to techniques for creating audio and video stories at www.genealogycenter.info/LifeStories/).
- Family Search article about oral history techniques www.familysearch.org/wiki/en/Creating_Oral_Histories.
- Family History Fanatics article about easy first steps for collecting family history stories at https://tinyurl.com/tkbef6v6.

## Put your PASS plan into action

No matter how you choose to bring family history alive, now is the time to put a PASS plan into action, in your own way. This is your opportunity to be sure the family's past survives.

As the family historian, you can tell the stories and show the photos even as you organize and analyze your genealogical collection, decide what to keep, and write instructions to keep your collection safe. Inch by inch, you'll make progress.

Good luck, and enjoy the journey!

## To sum up:

√    Know what interests your audience so you can gear your efforts accordingly.

√    Use photos to intrigue and inform.

√    Take a real or virtual field trip to places from your family's history.

√    Find the drama and tell the stories to make ancestors memorable.

√    Share family history through bite-sized projects that can be given to relatives and exchanged/posted digitally.

√    Reuse your content. Consider sharing on selected genealogy websites after reviewing the terms of service so you know how each site is legally allowed to use your content.

√     Put a PASS plan into action in your own way. Start now!

75

> ✓ **Prepare** to organize and analyze
> ✓ **Allocate** ownership by curating
> ✓ **Set up** a genealogical "will"
> ✓ **Share** your family's history now

# SAMPLE FORMS FOR YOUR PASS PROCESS

In this section are four sample forms you can use to organize, analyze, and plan a future for your family's history. Personalize and adapt any or all forms as needed to fit your own situation.

- Sample inventory (of a box, binder, folder) – discussed in Chapter 4

- Sample index (of a set of documents or photos) – discussed in Chapter 4

- Sample cousin connection chart - discussed in Chapter 8

- Sample genealogical "will" – discussed in Chapter 9

## SAMPLE INVENTORY

### Contents of Schaw #1 Box

(Tivador Schaw was Marian's paternal grandpa)
Inventoried on June 1, 2021 by Marian Wood

| *Item* | *Date* | *Place* | *Comments* |
|---|---|---|---|
| Schaw siblings in photo (size about 5" x 7"). Three sisters in fancy dress, one brother in Hungarian military uniform | 1915, June 1<br><br>Date on front | Ungvar, Hungary (now Uzhhorod, Ukraine) | Sepia, with handwritten inscription on reverse: "For dear Tivador" |
| Schaw, Tivador, U.S. naturalization certificate #214 | 1911, May 9<br><br>Date stamp | New York, New York, U.S.A. | Tivador was 24, blue eyes, brown hair, not married, living at 282 Avenue C, New York City |

Sortable and searchable by name, date, place.

## SAMPLE INDEX

### Index to Mac McClure diaries
### Updated by Marian Wood
### on May 12, 2021

Mac McClure, older son of Janice Brown McClure and Alexander McClure, kept a daily diary from 1959-1986. Diaries are in a box labeled "Mac McClure diaries," in Marian's home office.

| *Name* | *Relationship* | *Date* | *Place* | *Comments* |
|---|---|---|---|---|
| Brown, William (Billy) | Mac's first cousin on his mother's side. | 1964, Nov. 27 | Indiana, Wabash | Quote: "Drove to Wabash, Indiana, for Thanksgiving dinner with Billy. He showed slides of Brown reunion." |
| Surname, given (include nickname or maiden name) | Relationship | Year first | State or county first | Extra info |

Sortable and searchable by name, date, place. Add or delete columns depending on what is being indexed.

# SAMPLE COUSIN CONNECTION CHART

80

| NAME | CONTACT INFO | NOTES |
|---|---|---|
| **Surname, Given** (maiden name: ___) (relationship: ___) | 892 Street Name City, State, Country, Postal Code<br><br>Phone<br><br>Email | Daughter of Sally Sample. Her mother was at Marian's wedding in 19xx. Marian visited with her in 2019. |

Sortable by surname, and searchable by name, date, place.

# SAMPLE GENEALOGICAL "WILL"

To my spouse, children and/or heirs, guardian, administrator or executor:

Upon my death, it is requested that you DO NOT dispose of any or all of my genealogical records, both those prepared personally, and those prepared by others, which may be in my possession. This includes but is not limited to books, paper and/or computer files, notebooks, correspondence, audio/visual items, photographs, and documents, for a period of two years.

During this two-year period, please attempt to identify one or more persons who would be willing to take custody of said materials and the responsibility of maintaining and continuing the family histories.

Parties to contact regarding the assumption of the custody of these items include but are not limited to:

**NAME**    **ADDRESS**    **PHONE/EMAIL**

---

In the event that you find no one to accept these materials, please contact the institutions listed below, in order, and determine if they will accept part or all of my genealogical materials.

**INSTITUTION**  **ADDRESS/CONTACT**  **PHONE/EMAIL**

---

Please remember that my family history studies consumed a great deal of time, travel, and money. Therefore, it is my strong desire that the product of these efforts be preserved and allowed to continue in a manner that will make them available to others in the future.

Signature        Witness

__________________________  __________________________

(name)__________________  (name) __________________

Date __________________  Date __________________

NOTE: This sample genealogical "will" is adapted and reprinted with the kind permission of the *Devon Family History Society*.

# Remember the Pass Process

**Step 1:** Prepare to organize and analyze (Chapters 1-5)

**Step 2:** Allocate ownership (Chapters 6-7)

**Step 3:** Set up a genealogical "will" (Chapters 8-10)

**Step 4:** Share family history now (Chapter 11)

# INDEX